you'll
get
through
this

HOPE AND HELP FOR **YOUR TURBULENT** TIMES

MAX LUCADO

New York Times BESTSELLING AUTHOR

Praise for *You'll Get Through This*

"Max Lucado's latest book, *You'll Get Through This*, digs deep into what it means to go through hard times as a believer, and it gives a realistic, hopeful view of where God is in the process. Let's face it: life is tough sometimes, and it's easy to wonder where God is in the middle of a struggle. Max hits that head-on. As someone who has made a lot of mistakes and been through a lot of hard times, I'm really glad Max wrote this book."

—Dave Ramsey, *New York Times* best-selling author
and nationally syndicated radio show host

"It's popular for some Christian ministers to sell the magic elixir of 'believe and achieve,' which quickly dispatches our pain and problems and leaves us living the free and easy life. It's popular, but there is just one little issue—it's not true. Real faith doesn't get us *out* of trouble, just *through* it. Max Lucado is one of America's most trusted Christian authors because his messages speak to people who aren't living a fairy tale but a faith trail. This latest book is rooted in reality and in scripture. It will help you."

—Gov. Mike Huckabee, host of *Huckabee* on Fox News Channel, *The
Mike Huckabee Show* and the *Huckabee Report* on Cumulus Radio
Network; and five-time *New York Times* best-selling author

"Max Lucado has a genius for gently grabbing his readers in the first sentence and captivating them until the very last word. But it's what's on the pages in between that will move you to the very marrow: truth. In this newest book Max makes the four-thousand-year-old story of Joseph as relevant to you as today's headlines. You will definitely come away believing that 'you'll get through this'—whatever 'this' is in your life."

—Kathie Lee Gifford, cohost, the fourth hour of the *Today Show*

"When times are tough we all could use some reassurance. Like a tried and true friend, Max Lucado delivers biblical truth in encouraging fashion. His words will bring you relief in the present and hope for the future. *You'll Get Through This* will help you do just that. It's more than a title; it's a promise."

—Dave Stone, pastor, Southeast Christian Church

"Max Lucado blows a trumpet of victory as he takes you on a journey through the ruins of Joseph's life and his transformation into the second-most powerful man of his generation. As you recognize your own shattered dreams and broken heart through Joseph's journey, you will also learn to trust in God's unfailing truths."

—Janelle Hail, founder and CEO, National Breast Cancer Foundation, Inc.

"This is a life-changing message, shared at a critical time in the way only Max can. No matter what you are walking through, you will find hope and strength to stand when everything around you seems to be falling. Max gives us a profound reminder that God is in control."

—Sheila Walsh, author, *God Loves Broken People: And Those Who Pretend They're Not*; and Women of Faith® speaker

"Heavy-hearted people living in a heavy-handed world need more than wishful thinking going for them. That stuff might help us face a tough moment, but it can't get us beyond it. We need something huge, genuine, and reliable for that to happen. Fortunately, we worship a God who's in the hope business. Max Lucado captures the sound of His voice with all its glorious grace in *You'll Get Through This*. If life has knocked you down, this book will show you how to get back up and stay there."

—Dr. Tim Kimmel, author, *Grace-Based Parenting*

"We all encounter chapters in our personal stories when life doesn't go as we imagined it would. In his classic style Max Lucado draws from the biblical story of Joseph to encourage us that we'll get through it—and that God will redeem the hard times for His glory and purpose."

—Jim Daly, president, Focus on the Family

"Without doubt we are living in turbulent times. We long to know that our storms, trials, disappointments, and challenges have a purpose beyond our pain. In this book Max masterfully and compellingly shows us how our greatest trials and worst mistakes can be the launching pad into our destiny. Nothing is wasted. Don't give up. You'll get through this. I was riveted from the first word to the last."

—Christine Caine, founder, The A21 Campaign; and best-selling author, *Undaunted*

"As someone who has struggled and suffered, I know this message is not only true, it is utterly crucial. God doesn't want *anyone* to go through life without knowing this. *Please don't*."

—Eric Metaxas, *New York Times* best-selling author, *Bonhoeffer: Pastor, Martyr, Prophet, Spy* and *Amazing Grace: William Wilberforce and the Heroic Campaign to End Slavery*

"Max Lucado and Joseph the Coat-Wearer are a winning combination. I defy anybody to read this book and not be encouraged."

—John Ortberg, senior pastor, Menlo Park Presbyterian Church; and author, *Who Is This Man?*

"As the title itself says, this book is a must-read for anyone who has ever felt stuck or discouraged because of circumstances. Max doesn't just speak from personal experience but points us to the stories in scripture of God's faithfulness and reminds us that not a single follower has ever been deserted in life's journey. It is not just Max reassuring us but him showing us who God is—a rescuer, a deliverer, who delights in the redemption of His people."

—Laura Story, Grammy Award-winning artist and writer of the hit songs *Indescribable* and *Blessings*

"In his new book *You'll Get Through This*, Max offers much needed practical wisdom for those who are facing what seem like impossible obstacles. If you need comfort, encouragement, or hope, this book will reveal the faithfulness of God and give faith to believe that you'll get through this."

—Craig Groeschel, senior pastor, LifeChurch.tv; and author, *Altar Ego: Becoming Who God Says You Are*

"Every book by Max Lucado is an individual work of art, revealing profound truths through powerful prose and iridescent story. *You'll Get Through This* is no exception. Masterfully unfolding episodes from the life of Joseph, this book leaves you with an overwhelming sense of confidence that His presence will take you through and His deep love will make you whole."

—Wayne Cordeiro, pastor, New Hope Christian Fellowship

"Sometimes I get as anxious as a long-tailed cat in a roomful of rocking chairs when I can't see around the corner of my circumstances. But in *You'll Get Through This*, Max reminded me that God is *always* in control *and* His providence will never take me to a place where His grace won't sustain me."

—Lisa Harper, Bible teacher, author, and Women of Faith® speaker

"Most of us know the story of the multi-colored coat, the dreams, and the jealous brothers. We know how Joseph ended up in the bottom of a cistern, and we may even remember how Joseph got out. But many of us have missed how Joseph's story mirrors our own. We're all facing a pit, aren't we? In *You'll Get Through This* Max Lucado offers practical advice that is both sage and compassionate. It's a reminder that the God who redeemed Joseph's story is redeeming each of ours."

—Mark Batterson, *New York Times* best-selling author, *The Circle Maker*

"From time to time each of us confronts 'trials, toils, and snares.' In this uplifting new book Max Lucado inspiringly provides comfort and hope for our darkest moments. In his inimitable way Max weaves Joseph's powerful story of faithful endurance into our own, calling us to lean on God's promises as He carries us through the valley of shadows and into a bright new day."

—Kenneth Winston Starr, president, Baylor University

"No matter how bleak our reality, God is bigger still. And because He is good and motivated by intense love for each of us, God can and will lead us up the mountain of adversity and through the valley of the shadow of death. His presence will be enough as He flexes His might and uses the pain for greater good and eternal glory. And who better to lead us into these assuring truths? None other than Max Lucado. Only his pastoral heart rivals his writing genius, and the two together will shepherd you forward with the confidence that *you'll get through this*. Read this book and let Jesus use Max to lead you through the most turbulent times."

—Louie Giglio, pastor, Passion City Church/Passion Conferences; and author, *I Am Not but I Know I AM*

"I can speak from my own life, that my trials and tribulations have taught me so much more about the sweetness of Christ than my affluence and 'happy' times ever have. God is teaching us and preparing us for His true plan for our lives through the trials and tribulations of this fallen world. Max does a superb job, using the story of Joseph to show all of us that God will carry us through, not just to survive but to find our true calling in His divine plan."

"Max Lucado still delivers. His writing is required reading! *You'll Get Through This* provides encouragement, a sense of direction, and, ultimately, a real and needed dose of hope. I highly recommend it."

you'll
get
through
this

ALSO BY MAX LUCADO

you'll get through this

HOPE AND HELP FOR YOUR TURBULENT TIMES

MAX LUCADO

THOMAS NELSON
Since 1798

Published in Nashville, Tennessee, by Thomas Nelson. Thomas Nelson is a registered trademark of Thomas Nelson, Inc.

Thomas Nelson, Inc. titles may be purchased in bulk for educational, business, fund-raising, or sales promotional use. For information, please e-mail SpecialMarkets@ThomasNelson.com.

ISBN: 978-0-7180-8221-5 (custom)
ISBN: 978-0-7180-3151-0 (TP)
ISBN: 978-1-4003-7926-2 (IE)

Library of Congress Cataloging-in-Publication Data

Lucado, Max.
  You'll get through this : hope and help for your turbulent times / Max Lucado.
    pages cm
  Includes bibliographical references.
  ISBN 978-0-8499-4847-3
  1. Joseph (Son of Jacob) 2. Suffering—Religious aspects—Christianity. I. Title.
  BS580.J6L78 2013
  248.8'6—dc23   2013006953

Printed in the United States of America

15 16 17 18 19 RRD 6 5 4 3 2 1

For Cheryl Green
Steady, wise, full of joy and faith.
Thank you for the innumerable hours of service you
have given to the UpWords ministry and the Oak
Hills Church. You model servanthood.

Contents

Acknowledgments

Liz Heaney and Karen Hill, editors supreme. I can never thank you enough for your hours upon hours of dedication.

The publishing team of David Moberg, Paula Major, Liz Johnson, LeeEric Fesko, Greg and Susan Ligon, and Jana Muntsinger and Pamela McClure. Time and time again you stun us with your creativity and selfless service.

Steve Green and his wife, Cheryl, to whom this book is dedicated. You never seek applause. You always defer the credit. Yet those of us who depend on you know that we would sink like a rock without your contribution.

Carol Bartley, copy editor. Between you and God's grace, all my mistakes are blotted out! You set the standard, dear friend. So glad you are on this team.

Our Oak Hills Church senior minister, Randy Frazee, and our executive minister, Mark Tidwell. I am honored to call you friends.

The Oak Hills Church. The release of this book coincides with the twenty-fifth anniversary of our service together. May God grant us twenty-five more!

Elder David Treat. A special thank-you for your prayers and pastoral presence.

Margaret Mechinus, Tina Chisholm, Ashley Rosales, and Janie Padilla. You keep keen eyes on everything from correspondence to book orders. Once again, gracias!

David Drury. You are always a phone call or an e-mail away. Your theological mind is a blessing.

Since this is my thirtieth nonfiction book, it is appropriate to thank bookstores, both online and on the street, for three decades of partnership.

And my daughters and son-in-law, Jenna, Brett, Andrea, and Sara. You are first in my heart and thoughts.

And Denalyn, my dear wife. You are a candle to my cavern, ever warm and bright. I love you.

CHAPTER 1

you'll get through this

She had a tremble to her, the inner tremble you could feel with just a hand on her shoulder. I saw her in a grocery store. Had not seen her in some months. I asked about her kids and husband, and when I did, her eyes watered, her chin quivered, and the story spilled out. He'd left her. After twenty years of marriage, three kids, and a dozen moves, gone. Traded her in for a younger model. She did her best to maintain her composure but couldn't. The grocery store produce section became a sanctuary of sorts. Right there between the tomatoes and the heads of lettuce, she wept. We prayed. Then I said, "You'll get through this. It won't be painless. It won't be quick. But God will use this mess for good. In the meantime don't be foolish or naive. But don't despair either. With God's help you will get through this."

Two days later a friend called. He'd just been fired. The dismissal was his fault. He'd made stupid, inappropriate remarks at work. Crude, offensive statements. His boss kicked him out. Now he's a fifty-seven-year-old unemployed manager in a rotten economy. He feels terrible and sounds worse. Wife angry. Kids confused. He needed assurance, so I gave it: "You'll get through this. It won't be painless. It won't be quick. But God will use this mess for good. In the meantime don't be foolish or naive. But don't despair either. With God's help you will get through this."

Then there is the teenager I met at the café where she works.

She's fresh out of high school, hoping to get into college next month. Her life, as it turns out, hasn't been easy. When she was six years old, her parents divorced. When she was fifteen, they remarried, only to divorce again a few months ago. Recently her parents told her to choose: live with Mom or live with Dad. She got misty-eyed as she described their announcement. I didn't have a chance to tell her this, but if I see her again, you can bet your sweet September I am going to look her square in the eyes and say, "You'll get through this. It won't be painless. It won't be quick. But God will use this mess for good. In the meantime don't be foolish or naive. But don't despair either. With God's help you will get through this."

Audacious of me, right? How dare I say such words? Where did I get the nerve to speak such a promise into tragedy? In a pit, actually. A deep, dark pit. So steep, the boy could not climb out. Had he been able to, his brothers would have shoved him back down. They were the ones who had thrown him in.

> So it came to pass, when Joseph had come to his brothers, that they stripped Joseph of his tunic, the tunic of many colors that was on him. Then they took him and cast him into a pit. And the pit was empty; there was no water in it.
>
> And they sat down to eat a meal. (Gen. 37:23–25)

It was an abandoned cistern. Jagged rocks and roots extended from its sides. The seventeen-year-old boy lay at the bottom. Downy beard, spindly arms and legs. His hands were bound, ankles tied. He lay on his side, knees to chest, cramped in the small space. The sand was wet with spittle, where he had drooled. His eyes were wide with fear. His voice was hoarse from screaming. It wasn't that his brothers didn't hear him. Twenty-two years later, when a famine had tamed their swagger and guilt had dampened their pride, they would confess, "We saw the anguish of his soul when he pleaded with us, and we would not hear" (42:21).

These are the great-grandsons of Abraham. The sons of Jacob. Couriers of God's covenant to a galaxy of people. Tribes will bear their banners. The name of Jesus Christ will appear on their family tree. They are the Scriptures' equivalent of royalty. Yet on this day they were the Bronze Age version of a dysfunctional family. They could have had their own reality TV show. In the shadow of a sycamore, in earshot of Joseph's appeals, they chewed on venison and passed the wineskin. Cruel and oafish. Hearts as hard as the Canaanite desert. Lunch mattered more than their brother. They despised the boy. "They hated him and could not speak peaceably to him . . . they hated him even more . . . they hated him . . . his brothers envied him" (37:4–5, 8, 11).

Here's why. Their father pampered Joseph like a prized calf. Jacob had two wives, Leah and Rachel, but one love, Rachel. When Rachel died, Jacob kept her memory alive by fawning over their first son. The brothers worked all day. Joseph played all day. They wore clothes from a secondhand store. Jacob gave Joseph a hand-stitched, multicolored cloak with embroidered sleeves. They slept in the bunkhouse. He had a queen-sized bed in his own room. While they ran the family herd, Joseph, Daddy's little darling, stayed home. Jacob treated the eleventh-born like a firstborn. The brothers spat at the sight of Joseph.

To say the family was in crisis would be like saying a grass hut might be unstable in a hurricane.

The brothers caught Joseph far from home, sixty miles away from Daddy's protection, and went nuclear on him. "They *stripped* Joseph of his tunic . . . they *took* him and *cast* him into a pit" (vv. 23–24).[1] Defiant verbs. They wanted not only to kill Joseph but also hide his body. This was a murderous cover-up from the get-go. "We shall say, 'Some wild beast has devoured him'" (v. 20).

Joseph didn't see this assault coming. He didn't climb out of bed that morning and think, *I'd better dress in padded clothing because this is the day I get tossed into a hole.* The attack caught him off guard.

So did yours. Joseph's pit came in the form of a cistern. Maybe yours came in the form of a diagnosis, a foster home, or a traumatic injury. Joseph was thrown in a hole and despised. And you? Thrown in an unemployment line and forgotten. Thrown into a divorce and abandoned, into a bed and abused. The pit. A kind of death, waterless and austere. Some people never recover. Life is reduced to one quest: get out and never be hurt again. Not simply done. Pits have no easy exits.

Joseph's story got worse before it got better. Abandonment led to enslavement, then entrapment, and finally imprisonment. He was sucker punched. Sold out. Mistreated. People made promises only to break them, offered gifts only to take them back. If hurt were a swampland, then Joseph was sentenced to a life of hard labor in the Everglades.

Yet he never gave up. Bitterness never staked its claim. Anger never metastasized into hatred. His heart never hardened; his resolve never vanished. He not only survived; he thrived. He ascended like a helium balloon. An Egyptian official promoted him to chief servant. The prison warden placed him over the inmates. And Pharaoh, the highest ruler on the planet, shoulder-tapped Joseph to serve as his prime minister. By the end of his life, Joseph was the second most powerful man of his generation. It is not hyperbole to state that he saved the world from starvation. How would that look on a résumé?

Joseph
Son of Jacob
Graduate with honors from the University of Hard Knocks
Director of Global Effort to Save Humanity
Succeeded

How? How did he flourish in the midst of tragedy? We don't have to speculate. Some twenty years later the roles were reversed, Joseph as the strong one and his brothers the weak ones. They came to him in dread. They feared he would settle the score and throw them into a pit of his own making. But Joseph didn't. And in his explanation we find his inspiration.

> As for you, you meant evil against me, but God meant it for good in order to bring about this present result, to preserve many people alive. (50:20 NASB)

In God's hands intended evil becomes eventual good.

Joseph tied himself to the pillar of this promise and held on for dear life. Nothing in his story glosses over the *presence* of evil. Quite the contrary. Bloodstains, tearstains are everywhere. Joseph's heart was rubbed raw against the rocks of disloyalty and miscarried justice. Yet time and time again God redeemed the pain. The torn robe became a royal one. The pit became a palace. The broken family grew old together. The very acts intended to destroy God's servant turned out to strengthen him.

"You *meant* evil against me," Joseph told his brothers, using a Hebrew verb that traces its meaning to "weave" or "plait."[2] "You *wove* evil," he was saying, "but God *rewove* it together for good."

God, the Master Weaver. He stretches the yarn and intertwines the colors, the ragged twine with the velvet strings, the pains with the pleasures. Nothing escapes his reach. Every king, despot, weather pattern, and molecule are at his command. He passes the shuttle back and forth across the generations, and as he does, a design emerges. Satan weaves; God reweaves.

And God, the Master Builder. This is the meaning behind Joseph's words "God meant it for good in order to *bring about . . .*"[3] The

Hebrew word translated here as *bring about* is a construction term.[4] It describes a task or building project akin to the one I drive through every morning. The state of Texas is rebuilding a highway overpass near my house. Three lanes have been reduced to one, transforming a morning commute into a daily stew. The interstate project, like human history, has been in development since before time began. Cranes hover overhead daily. Workers hold signs and shovels, and several million of us grumble. Well, at least I do. *How long is this going to last?*

My next-door neighbors have a different attitude toward the project. The husband and wife are highway engineers, consultants to the department of transportation. They endure the same traffic jams and detours as the rest of us but do so with a better attitude. Why? They know how these projects develop. "It will take time," they respond to my grumbles, "but it will get finished. It's doable." They've seen the plans.

By giving us stories like Joseph's, God allows us to study his plans. Such disarray! Brothers dumping brother. Entitlements. Famines and family feuds scattered about like nails and cement bags on a vacant lot. Satan's logic was sinister and simple: destroy the family of Abraham and thereby destroy his seed, Jesus Christ. All of hell, it seems, set its target on Jacob's boys.

But watch the Master Builder at work. He cleared debris, stabilized the structure, and bolted trusses until the chaos of Genesis 37:24 ("They . . . cast him into a pit") became the triumph of Genesis 50:20 ("life for many people").[5]

God as Master Weaver, Master Builder. He redeemed the story of Joseph. Can't he redeem your story as well?

You'll get through this. You fear you won't. We all do. We fear that the depression will never lift, the yelling will never stop, the pain will never leave. Here in the pits, surrounded by steep walls and angry brothers, we wonder, *Will this gray sky ever brighten? This load ever lighten?* We feel stuck, trapped, locked in. Predestined for failure. Will we ever exit this pit?

Yes! Deliverance is to the Bible what jazz music is to Mardi Gras: bold, brassy, and everywhere.

Out of the lions' den for Daniel, the prison for Peter, the whale's belly for Jonah, Goliath's shadow for David, the storm for the disciples, disease for the lepers, doubt for Thomas, the grave for Lazarus, and the shackles for Paul. God gets us through stuff. *Through* the Red Sea onto dry ground (Ex. 14:22), *through* the wilderness (Deut. 29:5), *through* the valley of the shadow of death (Ps. 23:4), and *through* the deep sea (Ps. 77:19). *Through* is a favorite word of God's:

> When you pass *through* the waters, I will be with you;
> And *through* the rivers, they shall not overflow you.
> When you walk *through* the fire, you shall not be burned,
> Nor shall the flame scorch you. (Isa. 43:2)[6]

It won't be painless. Have you wept your final tear or received your last round of chemotherapy? Not necessarily. Will your unhappy marriage become happy in a heartbeat? Not likely. Are you exempt from any trip to the cemetery? Does God guarantee the absence of struggle and the abundance of strength? Not in this life. But he does pledge to reweave your pain for a higher purpose.

It won't be quick. Joseph was seventeen years old when his brothers abandoned him. He was at least thirty-seven when he saw them again. Another couple of years passed before he saw his father.[7] Sometimes God takes his time: One hundred twenty years to prepare Noah for the flood, eighty years to prepare Moses for his work. God called young David to be king but returned him to the sheep pasture. He called Paul to be an apostle and then isolated him in Arabia for perhaps three years. Jesus was on the earth for three decades before he built anything more than a kitchen table. How long will God take with you? He may take his time. His history is redeemed not in minutes but in lifetimes.

But God will use your mess for good. We see a perfect mess; God sees a perfect chance to train, test, and teach the future prime minister. We see a prison; God sees a kiln. We see famine; God sees the relocation of his chosen lineage. We call it Egypt; God calls it protective custody, where the sons of Jacob can escape barbaric Canaan and multiply abundantly in peace. We see Satan's tricks and ploys. God sees Satan tripped and foiled.

Let me be clear. You are a version of Joseph in your generation. You represent a challenge to Satan's plan. You carry something of God within you, something noble and holy, something the world needs—wisdom, kindness, mercy, skill. If Satan can neutralize you, he can mute your influence.

The story of Joseph is in the Bible for this reason: to teach you to trust God to trump evil. What Satan intends for evil, God, the Master Weaver and Master Builder, redeems for good.

Joseph would be the first to tell you that life in the pit stinks. Yet for all its rottenness doesn't the pit do this much? It forces you to look upward. Someone from *up there* must come *down here* and give you a hand. God did for Joseph. At the right time, in the right way, he will do the same for you.

CHAPTER 2

down, down, down to egypt

Joseph's troubles started when his mouth did. He came to breakfast one morning, bubbling and blabbing in sickening detail about the images he had seen in his sleep: sheaves of wheat lying in a circle, all bundled up, ready for harvest. Each one tagged with the name of a different brother—Reuben, Gad, Levi, Zebulun, Judah . . . Right in the center of the circle was Joseph's sheaf. In his dream only his sheaf stood up. The implication: you will bow down to me.

Did he expect his brothers to be excited about this? To pat him on the back and proclaim, "We will gladly kneel before you, our dear baby brother"? They didn't. They kicked dust in his face and told him to get lost.

He didn't take the hint. He came back with another dream. Instead of sheaves it was now stars, a sun, and a moon. The stars represented the brothers. The sun and moon symbolized Joseph's father and deceased mother. All were bowing to Joseph. Joseph! The kid with the elegant coat and soft skin. They, bow down to him?

He should have kept his dreams to himself.

Perhaps Joseph was thinking that very thing as he sat in the bottom of that cistern. His calls for help hadn't done any good. His brothers had seized the chance to seize and silence him once and for all.

But from deep in the pit, Joseph detected a new sound—the sound of a wagon and a camel, maybe two. Then a new set of voices.

Foreign. They spoke to the brothers with an accent. Joseph strained to understand the conversation.

"We'll sell him to you . . ."

"How much?"

" . . . trade for your camels . . ."

Joseph looked up to see a circle of faces staring down at him.

Finally one of the brothers was lowered into the pit on the end of a rope. He wrapped both arms around Joseph, and the others pulled them out.

The traders examined Joseph from head to toe. They stuck fingers in his mouth and counted his teeth. They pinched his arms for muscle. The brothers made their pitch: "Not an ounce of fat on those bones. Strong as an ox. He can work all day."

The merchants huddled, and when they came back with an offer, Joseph realized what was happening. "Stop this! Stop this right now! I am your brother! You can't sell me!" His brothers shoved him to the side and began to barter.

"What will you pay for him?"

"We'll give you ten coins."

"No less than thirty."

"Fifteen and no more."

"Twenty-five."

"Twenty, and that is our last offer."

The brothers took the coins, grabbed the fancy coat, and walked away. Joseph fell on his knees and wailed. The merchants tied one end of a rope around his neck and the other to the wagon. Joseph, dirty and tearstained, had no choice but to follow. He fell in behind the creaking wagon and the rack-ribbed camels. He cast one final glance over his shoulder at the backs of his brothers, who disappeared over the horizon.

"Help me!"

No one turned around.

"His brothers . . . sold him for twenty pieces of silver to the Ishmaelites who took Joseph with them down to Egypt" (Gen. 37:28 MSG).

Down to Egypt. Just a few hours ago Joseph's life was looking up. He had a new coat and a pampered place in the house. He dreamed his brothers and parents would look up to him. But what goes up must come down, and Joseph's life came down with a crash. Put down by his siblings. Thrown down into an empty well. Let down by his brothers and sold down the river as a slave. Then led down the road to Egypt.

Down, down, down. Stripped of name, status, position. Everything he had, everything he thought he'd ever have—gone. Vanished. Poof. Just like that.

Just like you? Have you been down in the mouth, down to your last dollar, down to the custody hearing, down to the bottom of the pecking order, down on your luck, down on your life . . . down . . . down to Egypt?

Life pulls us down.

Joseph arrived in Egypt with nothing. Not a penny to his name or a name worth a penny. His family tree was meaningless. His occupation was despised.[1] The clean-shaven people of the pyramids avoided the woolly bedouins of the desert.

No credentials to stand on. No vocation to call on. No family to lean on. He had lost everything, with one exception. His destiny.

Those odd dreams had convinced Joseph that God had plans for him. The details were vague and ill defined, for sure. Joseph had no way of knowing the specifics of his future. But the dreams told him this much: he would have a place of prominence in the midst of his family. Joseph latched on to this dream for the life jacket it was.

How else do we explain his survival? The Bible says nothing

about his training, education, superior skills, or talents. But the narrator made a lead story out of Joseph's destiny.

The Hebrew boy lost his family, dignity, and home country, but he never lost his belief in God's belief in him. Trudging through the desert toward Egypt, he resolved, *It won't end this way. God has a dream for my life.* While wearing the heavy chains of the slave owners, he remembered, *I've been called to more than this.* Dragged into a city of strange tongues and shaved faces, he told himself, *God has greater plans for me.*

God had a destiny for Joseph, and the boy believed in it.

Do you believe in God's destiny for you?

I'm entering my fourth decade as a pastor. Thirty years is plenty of time to hear Joseph stories. I've met many Egypt-bound people. Down, down, down. I've learned the question to ask. If you and I were having this talk over coffee, this is the point where I would lean across the table and say, "What do you still have that you cannot lose?" The difficulties have taken much away. I get that. But there is one gift your troubles cannot touch: your destiny. Can we talk about it?

You are God's child. He saw you, picked you, and placed you. "You did not choose me; I chose you" (John 15:16 NCV). Before you are a butcher, baker, or cabinetmaker, male or female, Asian or black, you are God's child. Replacement or fill-in? Hardly. You are his first choice.

Such isn't always the case in life. Once, just minutes before I officiated at a wedding, the groom leaned over to me and said, "You weren't my first choice."

"I wasn't?"

"No, the preacher I wanted couldn't make it."

"Oh."

"But thanks for filling in."

"Sure. Anytime." I considered signing the marriage license "Substitute."

You'll never hear such words from God. He chose you. The choice wasn't obligatory, required, compulsory, forced, or compelled. He selected you because he wanted to. You are his open, willful, voluntary choice. He walked onto the auction block where you stood, and he proclaimed, "This child is mine." And he bought you "with the precious blood of Christ, as of a lamb without blemish and without spot" (1 Peter 1:19). You are God's child.

You are his child *forever*.

Don't believe the tombstone. You are more than a dash between two dates. "When this tent we live in—our body here on earth—is torn down, God will have a house in heaven for us to live in, a home he himself has made, which will last forever" (2 Cor. 5:1 TEV). Don't get sucked into short-term thinking. Your struggles will not last forever, but you will.

God will have his Eden. He is creating a garden in which Adams and Eves will share in his likeness and love, at peace with each other, animals, and nature. We will rule with him over lands, cities, and nations. "If we endure, we shall also reign with Him" (2 Tim. 2:12).

Believe this. Clutch it. Tattoo it on the interior of your heart. It may seem that the calamity sucked your life out to sea, but it hasn't. You still have your destiny.

My father walked the road to Egypt. Family didn't betray him; his health did. He had just retired. He and Mom had saved their money and made their plans. They wanted to visit every national park in their travel trailer. Then came the diagnosis: amyotrophic lateral sclerosis (ALS or Lou Gehrig's disease), a cruel degenerative disease that affects the muscles. Within months he was unable to feed, dress, or bathe himself. His world, as he knew it, was gone.

At the time my wife, Denalyn, and I were preparing to do mission work in Brazil. When we got the news, I offered to change my plans. How could I leave the country while he was dying? Dad's reply was immediate and confident. He was not known for his long letters, but this one took up four pages and included the following imperative.

> In regard to my disease and your going to Rio. That is really an easy answer for me, and that is *Go* . . . I have no fear of death or eternity . . . so don't be concerned about me. Just *Go*. Please him.

Dad lost much: his health, retirement, years with his children and grandchildren, years with his wife. The loss was severe, but it wasn't complete. "Dad," I could have asked, "what do you have that you cannot lose?" He still had God's call on his heart.

We forget this on the road to Egypt. Forgotten destinies litter the landscape like carcasses. We redefine ourselves according to our catastrophes. "I am the divorcée, the addict, the bankrupt business-person, the kid with the disability, or the man with the scar." We settle for a small destiny: to make money, make friends, make a name, make muscle, or make love with anyone and everyone.

Determine not to make this mistake. Think you have lost it all? You haven't. "God's gifts and God's call are under full warranty—never canceled, never rescinded" (Rom. 11:29 MSG). Hear and heed yours.

Here's how it works. Your company is laying off employees. Your boss finally calls you into his office. As kind as he tries to be, a layoff is a layoff. All of a sudden you are cleaning out your desk. Voices of doubt and fear raise their volume. *How will I pay the bills? Who is going to hire me?* Dread dominates your thoughts. But then you remember your destiny: *What do I have that I cannot lose?*

Wait a second. I am still God's child. My life is more than this life. These days are a vapor, a passing breeze. This will eventually pass.

God will make something good out of this. I will work hard, stay faithful, and trust him no matter what.

Bingo. You just trusted your destiny.

Try this one. Your fiancé wants his engagement ring back. All those promises and the proposal melted the moment he met the new girl at work. The jerk. The bum. The no-good pond scum. Like Joseph, you've been dumped into the pit. And, like Joseph, you choose to heed the call of God on your life. It's not easy. You're tempted to get even. But you choose instead to ponder your destiny. *I am God's child. My life is more than this life . . . more than this broken heart. This is God's promise, and unlike that sorry excuse for a guy, God won't break a promise.*

Another victory for God.

Survival in Egypt begins with a yes to God's call on your life.

Several years after Dad's death I received a letter from a woman who remembered him. Ginger was only six years old when her Sunday school class made get-well cards for ailing church members. She created a bright purple card out of construction paper and carefully lined it with stickers. On the inside she wrote, "I love you, but most of all God loves you." Her mom baked a pie, and the two made the delivery.

Dad was bedfast. The end was near. His jaw tended to drop, leaving his mouth open. He could extend his hand, but it was bent to a claw from the disease.

Somehow Ginger had a moment alone with him and asked a question as only a six-year-old can: "Are you going to die?"

He touched her hand and told her to come near. "Yes, I am going to die. When? I don't know."

She asked if he was afraid to go away. "Away is heaven," he told her. "I will be with my Father. I am ready to see him eye to eye."

About this point in the visit, her mother and mine returned. Ginger recalls:

My mother consoled your parents with a fake smile on her face. But I smiled a big, beautiful, *real* smile, and he did the same and winked at me.

My purpose for telling you all this is my family and I are going to Kenya. We are going to take Jesus to a tribe on the coast. I am very scared for my children, because I know there will be hardships and disease. But for me, I am not afraid, because the worst thing that could happen is getting to see "my Father eye to eye."

It was your father who taught me that earth is only a passing through and death is merely a rebirth.

A man near death winking at the thought of it. Stripped of everything? It only appeared that way. In the end Dad still had what no one could take. And in the end that is all he needed.

CHAPTER 3

alone but not all alone

Melanie Jasper says her son, Cooper, was born with a smile on his face. The dimple never left his cheek. He won the hearts of every person he knew: his three older sisters, parents, grandparents, teachers, and friends. He loved to laugh and love. His father, JJ, confessing partiality, calls him practically a perfect child.

And Cooper was born to the perfect family. Farm-dwelling, fun-loving, God-seeking, and Christ-hungry, JJ and Melanie poured their hearts into their four children. JJ cherished every moment he had with his only son. That's why they were riding in the dune buggy on July 17, 2009. They intended to cut the grass together, but the lawn mower needed a spark plug. While Melanie drove to town to buy one, JJ and five-year-old Cooper seized the opportunity for a quick ride. They had done this a thousand times, zipping down a dirt road in a roll cage cart. The ride was nothing new. But the flip was. On a completely level road with Cooper safely buckled in, JJ made a circle, and the buggy rolled over.

Cooper was unresponsive. JJ called 911, then Melanie. "There has been an accident," he told her. "I don't think Cooper is going to make it." The next hours were every parent's worst nightmare: ambulance, ER, sobs, and shock. And finally the news. Cooper had passed from this life into heaven. JJ and Melanie found themselves doing the unthinkable: selecting a casket, planning a funeral, and envisioning life without their only son. In the coming days they fell into a mind-numbing rhythm. Each morning upon awakening they held each other and sobbed uncontrollably. After gathering enough courage to climb out of bed, they would go downstairs to the family and friends who awaited them. They would soldier through the day until bedtime. Then they would go to bed, hold each other, and cry themselves to sleep.

JJ told me, "There is no class or book on this planet that can prepare you to have your five-year-old son die in your arms . . . We know what the bottom looks like."[1]

The bottom. We pass much of life—if not most of life—at mid-altitude. Occasionally we summit a peak: our wedding, a promotion, the birth of a child. But most of life is lived at midlevel. Mondayish obligations of carpools, expense reports, and recipes.

But on occasion the world bottoms out. The dune buggy flips, the housing market crashes, the test results come back positive, and before we know it, we discover what the bottom looks like.

In Joseph's case he discovered what the auction block of Egypt looked like. The bidding began, and for the second time in his young life, he was on the market. The favored son of Jacob found himself prodded and pricked, examined for fleas, and pushed about like a donkey. Potiphar, an Egyptian officer, bought him. Joseph didn't speak the language or know the culture. The food was strange, the work was grueling, and the odds were against him.

So we turn the page and brace for the worst. The next chapter in his story will describe Joseph's consequential plunge into addiction, anger, or despair, right? Wrong.

"The LORD was with Joseph, and he was a successful man; and he was in the house of his master the Egyptian" (Gen. 39:2). Joseph arrived in Egypt with nothing but the clothes on his back and the call of God on his heart. Yet by the end of four verses, he was running the house of the man who ran security for Pharaoh. How do we explain this turnaround? Simple. God was with him.

> The LORD was with Joseph, and he was a successful man. (v. 2)

> His master saw that the LORD was with him. (v. 3)

> The LORD blessed the Egyptian's house for Joseph's sake. (v. 5)

> The blessing of the LORD was on all that he had. (v. 5)

Joseph's story just parted company with the volumes of self-help books and all the secret-to-success formulas that direct the struggler to an inner power ("dig deeper"). Joseph's story points elsewhere ("look higher"). He succeeded because God was present. God was to Joseph what a blanket is to a baby—he was all over him.

Any chance he'd be the same for you? Here you are in your version of Egypt. It feels foreign. You don't know the language. You never studied the vocabulary of crisis. You feel far from home, all alone. Money gone. Expectations dashed. Friends vanished. Who's left? God is.

David asked, "Where can I go to get away from your Spirit? Where can I run from you?" (Ps. 139:7 NCV). He then listed the various places he found God: in "the heavens . . . the grave . . . If I rise with the sun in the east and settle in the west beyond the sea, even there you would guide me" (vv. 8–10 NCV). God, everywhere.

Joseph's account of those verses would have read, "Where can I go to get away from your Spirit? If I go to the bottom of the dry pit . . . to the top of the slave block . . . to the home of a foreigner . . . even there you would guide me."

Your adaptation of the verse might read, "Where can I go to get away from your Spirit? If I go to the rehab clinic . . . the ICU . . . the overseas deployment office . . . the shelter for battered women . . . the county jail . . . even there you would guide me."

You will never go where God is not. Envision the next few hours of your life. Where will you find yourself? In a school? God indwells the classroom. On the highways? His presence lingers among the traffic. In the hospital operating room, the executive boardroom, the in-laws' living room, the funeral home? God will be there. "He is not far from each one of us" (Acts 17:27).

Each of us. God does not play favorites. From the masses on the city avenues to the isolated villagers in valleys and jungles, all people can enjoy God's presence. But many don't. They plod through life as if there were no God to love them. As if their only strength was their own. As if the only solution comes from within, not above. They live God-less lives.

But there are Josephs among us: people who sense, see, and hear the presence of God. People who pursue God as Moses did. When suddenly tasked with the care of two million ex-slaves, the liberator began to wonder, *How am I going to provide for these people? How will we defend ourselves against enemies? How can we survive?* Moses needed supplies, managers, equipment, and experience. But when Moses prayed for help, he declared, "If Your Presence does not go with us, do not bring us up from here" (Ex. 33:15).

Moses preferred to go nowhere with God than anywhere without him.

As did David. The king ended up in an Egypt of his own making. He seduced the wife of a soldier and covered up his sin with murder and deceit. He hid from God for a year, but he could not hide forever. When he finally confessed his immorality, he made only one request of God: "Do not cast me away from Your presence, and do not take Your Holy Spirit from me" (Ps. 51:11).

David did not pray, "Do not take my crown from me. Do not take my kingdom from me. Do not take my army from me." David knew what mattered most. The presence of God. He begged God for it.

Do likewise. Make God's presence your passion. How? Be more sponge and less rock. Place a rock in the ocean, and what happens? Its surface gets wet. The exterior may change color, but the interior remains untouched. Yet place a sponge in the ocean, and notice the change. It absorbs the water. The ocean penetrates every pore and alters the essence of the sponge.

God surrounds us in the same way the Pacific surrounds an ocean floor pebble. He is everywhere—above, below, on all sides. We choose our response—rock or sponge? Resist or receive? Everything within you says harden the heart. *Run from God; resist God; blame God.* But be careful. Hard hearts never heal. Spongy ones do. Open every pore of your soul to God's presence. Here's how.

Lay claim to the nearness of God. "Never will I leave you; never will I forsake you" (Heb. 13:5 NIV). In the Greek this passage has five negatives. It could be translated "I will not, not leave thee; neither will I not, not forsake thee."[2] Grip this promise like the parachute it is. Repeat it to yourself over and over until it trumps the voices of fear and angst. "The LORD your God is with you, he is mighty to save. He will take great delight in you, he will quiet you with his love, he will rejoice over you with singing" (Zeph. 3:17 NIV).

You may lose the *sense* of God's presence. Job did. "But if I go to the east, he is not there; if I go to the west, I do not find him. When he is at work in the north, I do not see him; when he turns to the south, I catch no glimpse of him" (Job 23:8–9 NIV). Job *felt* far from God. Yet in spite of his inability to feel God, Job resolved, "But he knows the way that I take; when he has tested me, I will come forth as gold" (v. 10 NIV). What gritty determination. Difficult days demand decisions of faith.

The psalmist determined:

> When I am afraid,
>   *I will trust* in you. (Ps. 56:3 NIV)[3]

> Why are you downcast, O my soul?
>   Why so disturbed within me?
> Put your hope in God,
>   for *I will yet praise* him. (Ps. 42:5 NIV)[4]

Don't equate the presence of God with a good mood or a pleasant temperament. God is near whether you are happy or not. Sometimes you have to take your feelings outside and give them a good talking-to.

Cling to his character. Quarry from your Bible a list of the deep qualities of God, and press them into your heart. My list reads like this: "He is still sovereign. He still knows my name. Angels still respond to his call. The hearts of rulers still yield at his bidding. The death of Jesus still saves souls. The Spirit of God still indwells saints. Heaven is still only heartbeats away. The grave is still temporary housing. God is still faithful. He is not caught off guard. He uses everything for his glory and my ultimate good. He uses tragedy to accomplish his will, and his will is right, holy, and perfect. Sorrow may come with the night, but joy comes with the morning. God bears fruit in the midst of affliction."

When JJ Jasper told his oldest daughter about Cooper's death, he prepared her by saying, "I need you to hold on to everything you know of who God is, because I have some really tough news to tell you." What valuable counsel!

In changing times lay hold of the unchanging character of God.

> When all around my soul gives way,
> He then is all my hope and stay.[5]

Pray your pain out. Pound the table. March up and down the lawn. It's time for tenacious, honest prayers. Angry at God? Disappointed with his strategy? Ticked off at his choices? Let him know it. Let him have it! Jeremiah did. This ancient prophet pastored Jerusalem during a time of economic collapse and political upheaval. Invasion. Disaster. Exile. Hunger. Death. Jeremiah saw it all. He so filled his devotions with complaints that his prayer journal is called Lamentations.

> [God] has led me and made me walk
> In darkness and not in light.
> Surely He has turned His hand against me
> Time and time again throughout the day.
>
> He has aged my flesh and my skin,
> And broken my bones.
> He has besieged me
> And surrounded me with bitterness and woe.
> He has set me in dark places
> Like the dead of long ago.
>
> He has hedged me in so that I cannot get out;
> He has made my chain heavy.
> Even when I cry and shout,
> He shuts out my prayer. (3:2–8)

Jeremiah infused five chapters with this type of fury. Summarize the bulk of his book with one line: this life is rotten! Why would God place Lamentations in the Bible? Might it be to convince you to follow Jeremiah's example?

Go ahead and file your grievance. "I pour out my complaint before him; I tell my trouble before him" (Ps. 142:2 ESV). God will not turn away at your anger. Even Jesus offered up prayers with "loud cries and tears" (Heb. 5:7 NIV). It is better to shake a fist at God than to turn your back on him. Augustine said, "How deep in the deep are they who do not cry out of the deep."[6]

Words might seem hollow and empty at first. You will mumble your sentences, fumble your thoughts. But don't quit. And don't hide.

Lean on God's people. Cancel your escape to the Himalayas. Forget the deserted island. This is no time to be a hermit. Be a barnacle on the boat of God's church. "For where two or three are gathered together in My name, *I am there* in the midst of them" (Matt. 18:20).[7]

Would the sick avoid the hospital? The hungry avoid the food pantry? The discouraged abandon God's Hope Distribution Center? Only at great risk. His people purvey his presence.

Moses and the Israelites once battled the Amalekites. The military strategy of Moses was a strange one. He commissioned Joshua to lead the fight in the valley below. Moses ascended the hill to pray. But he did not go alone. He took his two lieutenants, Aaron and Hur. While Joshua led the physical combat, Moses engaged in a spiritual fight. Aaron and Hur stood on either side of their leader to hold up his arms in the battle of prayer. The Israelites prevailed because Moses prayed. Moses prevailed because he had others to pray with him.

My wife did something similar. Years ago Denalyn battled a dark cloud of depression. Every day was gray. Her life was loud and busy— two kids in elementary school, a third in kindergarten, and a husband who didn't know how to get off the airplane and stay home. The days took their toll. Depression can buckle the knees of the best of us, but it can be especially difficult for the wife of a pastor. Congregants expect her to radiate joy and bite bullets. But Denalyn, to her credit, has never been one to play games. On a given Sunday when the depression was suffocating, she armed herself with honesty and went to church. *If people ask me how I am doing, I'm going to tell them.*

She answered each "How are you?" with a candid "Not well. I'm depressed. Will you pray for me?"

Casual chats became long conversations. Brief hellos became heartfelt moments of ministry. By the time she left the worship service, she had enlisted dozens of people to hold up her arms in the battle of prayer. She traces the healing of her depression to that Sunday morning service. She found God's presence amid God's people.

So did JJ. His hurts are still deep, but his faith is deeper still. Whenever he tells the story of losing Cooper, he says this: "We know what the bottom looks like, and we know who is waiting there—Jesus Christ."

He's waiting on you, my friend. If Joseph's story is any precedent, God can use Egypt to teach you that he is with you. Your family may be gone. Your supporters may have left. Your counselor may be silent. But God has not budged. His promise still stands: "I am with you and will watch over you wherever you go" (Gen. 28:15 NIV).

stupid won't fix stupid

The Fourth of July. Everything about the holiday was red, white, and blue. My face was red, the clouds were cotton white, and the sky was a brilliant blue. My redness came not from sunburn but humiliation. Denalyn had warned, "Remember, Max, the lake level is low." The depth finder had alerted: thirty feet, then ten, then five, and then three feet. The caution buoys bobbed up and down in the water. But did I listen to Denalyn? Pay attention to the depth radar? Take note of the shallow-water markers?

Who had time for such trivialities? My three teenage daughters and their friends were counting on my navigational skills for a Saturday of entertainment. I would not disappoint. Wearing sunglasses and a big-brimmed hat, I hammered the throttle, and off we went. *Zoom!* Then five minutes later, boom! I had driven the boat onto a sandbar.

Passengers lurched forward. I nearly fell out. Seven sets of eyes glared at me. A lesser man might have told everyone to get out and push the boat back into deep water. Not me. Not throttle-happy Max. No sir. I was captain of the outboard, sovereign of the lake. I would debank the boat the manly way. I shoved the throttle again.

The boat didn't budge.

"Max," Denalyn kindly opined, "you messed up." I raised the rudder. It was bent like a dog's ear. This time we had no choice. We pushed until we floated. When I started the engine, the boat vibrated like a three-wheeled jalopy. Our speed peaked out at five miles per hour. As we chug-chugged across the lake and the other vacationers stared and the teenagers sulked, I asked myself, *Well, Captain Max, what were you thinking?*

That was the problem. I *wasn't* thinking. Dumb became dumber because I treated a bad decision with a poor, impulsive choice. Forgivable in a boat. But in life?

Joseph was probably in his twenties when he crashed into, of all things, a sandbar of sexual temptation. When his brothers sold him into slavery, they likely assumed they had doomed him to hard labor and an early death. Instead, Joseph moved up the career ladder like a fireman after a cat. Potiphar, who promoted Joseph in his home, no doubt promoted Joseph among his circle of officials. He boasted about the Midas touch of this bright Hebrew boy who had made him a wealthy man.[1]

Joseph came to have clout. He could spend and hire, send and receive. Merchants reported to him, and other people noticed him. Most significantly, women noticed him. "Now Joseph was a very handsome and well-built young man" (Gen. 39:6 NLT). A Hollywood head turner, this guy—square jaw, wavy hair, and biceps that bulged every time he carried Mrs. Potiphar's tray. Which was often. She enjoyed the sight of him. "And it came to pass after these things that his master's wife cast longing eyes on Joseph, and she said, 'Lie with me'" (v. 7).

The first lady of the household made a play for the Hebrew slave. "Jo-eeey, how about a little sugar with my coffee?" Wink, wink. As she passed him in the hallway, she brushed up against his arm. As he brought dessert to the table, she touched his leg. By the clothes she wore, or didn't wear, she made it clear: "I'm yours for the taking, Joseph." She courted him "day by day" (v. 10). He had plenty of opportunities to consider the proposition. And reasons to accept it.

Wasn't she married to his master? And wasn't he obligated to obey the wishes of his owner, even if the wish was clandestine sex?

And it *would be* clandestine. No one would know. What happens in the bedroom stays in the bedroom, right?

Besides, a dalliance with the randy lady would give Joseph a chip in the political poker game, an ally at the top level. The end justified the means. And the means wasn't all that unpleasant. Powerful Potiphar had his pick of women. His wife was likely a jaw-dropper. Joseph didn't lose his manly urges when he lost his coat of many colors. A few moments in the arms of an attractive, willing lover? Joseph could use some relief.

Didn't he deserve some? These were lonely days: rejected by his family, twice bought and sold like livestock, far from home, far from friends. And the stress of managing Potiphar's household. Overseeing the terraced gardens and multitude of slaves. Mastering the peculiar protocol of official events. Joseph's job was draining. He could have justified his choice.

So can you. You've been jilted and bruised, sold out and turned away. Stranded on the sandbar of bad health, bad credit, bad luck. Few friends and fewer solutions. The hours are long, and the nights are longer. Mrs. (or Mr.) Potiphar comes along with a sultry offer. She slides her room key in your direction.

Or a friend slides a bottle in your direction. A coworker offers some drugs. You can pay some personal bills with company cash or stave off bankruptcy by embezzling funds. Justifications and rationalizations pop up like weeds after a summer rain. *No one would know. I won't get caught. I'm only human.*

Can we talk candidly for a moment? Egypt can be a cruddy place. No one disagrees with that. But Egypt can also be the petri dish for brainless decisions. Don't make matters worse by doing something you'll regret.

Joseph went on high alert. When Mrs. Potiphar dangled the bait, "he refused" (v. 8). He gave the temptress no time, no attention, no chitchat, no reason for hope. "He did not heed her, to lie with her or to be with her" (v. 10). When her number appeared on his cell phone, he did not answer. When she texted a question, he didn't respond. When she entered his office, he exited. He avoided her like the poison she was.

"[Potiphar] has committed all that he has to my hand," he announced (v. 8). To lie with her would be to sin against his master. How rare this resolve. In a culture that uses phrases like "consenting adults" and "sexual rights," we forget how immorality destroys the lives of people who aren't in the bedroom.

Years ago a friend gave me this counsel: "Make a list of all the lives you would affect by your sexual immorality." I did. Every so often I reread it. "Denalyn. My three daughters. My son-in-law. My yet-to-be-born grandchildren. Every person who has ever read one of my books or heard one of my sermons. My publishing team. Our church staff." The list reminds me: one act of carnality is a poor exchange for a lifetime of lost legacy.

Dads, would you intentionally break the arm of your child? Of course not. Such an action would violate every fiber of your moral being. Yet if you engage in sexual activity outside of your marriage, you will bring much more pain into the life of your child than would a broken bone.

Moms, would you force your children to sleep outside on a cold night? By no means. Yet if you involve yourself in an illicit affair, you will bring more darkness and chill into the lives of your children than a hundred winters.

And you, single man or woman. You wouldn't desecrate a Bible or make a mockery of a cross. Yet when you have unmarried sex, you disregard one of God's holy acts. "Do you not know that your body is the temple of the Holy Spirit who is in you?" (1 Cor. 6:19).

Actions have consequences. Joseph placed his loyalty above lusts. He honored his master . . .

And his *Master.* Joseph's primary concern was the preference of God. "How . . . can I do this great wickedness, and sin against God?" (Gen. 39:9).

The lesson we learn from Joseph is surprisingly simple: *do what pleases God.* Your coworkers want to include a trip to a gentleman's club on the evening agenda. What do you do? *Do what pleases God.* Your date invites you to conclude the evening with drinks at his apartment. How should you reply? *Do what pleases God.* Your friends hand you a joint of marijuana to smoke; your classmates show you a way to cheat; the Internet provides pornography to watch—ask yourself the question: How can I please God? "Do what is right as a sacrifice to the LORD and trust the LORD" (Ps. 4:5 NCV).

You don't fix a struggling marriage with an affair, a drug problem with more drugs, debt with more debt. You don't fix stupid with stupid. You don't get out of a mess by making another one. *Do what pleases God.* You will never go wrong doing what is right.

Thomas made this discovery. He in many ways was a modern-day Joseph. Born in 1899 to a Baptist pastor and a church pianist, Thomas was exposed to music early on. By the age of twelve he was imitating the jazz music of the African American community in the Deep South. In his late teens he went to Philadelphia and then to Chicago, where he played in speakeasies. Somewhere along the way he forgot his faith. He compromised in his lifestyle and turned away from the convictions of his youth. His talent opened the doors, but his conscience wouldn't let him rest. Long nights on the road left him exhausted and weary. A relative urged him to return to God. At the age of twenty-one, he did. He had an encounter with God that later led him to write: "My inner-being was thrilled. My soul was a deluge of divine rapture; my emotions were aroused; my heart was inspired to become a great singer and worker in the kingdom of the Lord."[2]

Young Thomas poured his energy into God-honoring music. Rhythm and blues met worship and praise. The result was a brand-new genre of toe-tapping, soul-lifting music. He took a position as a music director at a Chicago church. At the age of twenty-six Thomas met the love of his life and got married. He began a publishing company and founded the National Convention of Gospel Choirs and Choruses. He worked with some of the greatest singers in the history of gospel music, including Mahalia Jackson. By 1932, Thomas was enjoying the blessings of God at full throttle: happy marriage, growing ministry, first child on the way. Life was good.

But then the sandbar. One night after singing to a Saint Louis audience, he was handed a Western Union telegram. It read simply: "Your wife just died." She had passed away in childbirth. Thomas hurried back to Chicago, where his newborn son died the following day. The musician fell into a crevasse of grief. He avoided people and grew angry at God. "I just wanted to go back to the jazz world I knew so well. I felt God had done me an injustice. I didn't want to serve Him anymore or write gospel songs."[3]

He secluded himself, nursing his anger and sorrow. A friend seemed to know what he needed. He took Thomas to a neighborhood music school. That evening as the sun was setting, Thomas sat down at a piano and began to play . . . and pray. He poured out his heart to God, and what wonderful words they were.

> Precious Lord, take my hand,
> Lead me on, let me stand,
> I am tired, I am weak, I am worn;
> Through the storm, through the night,
> Lead me on to the light:
> Take my hand, precious Lord, lead me home.[4]

For the rest of his life, Thomas A. Dorsey testified that the Lord healed him that night as he sat at the piano. He went on to pen more than three thousand songs and become one of the most influential Christian songwriters of all time.[5] All because he reached out to God.

Do the same. Turbulent times will tempt you to forget God. Shortcuts will lure you. Sirens will call you. But don't be foolish or naive. Do what pleases God. Nothing more, nothing less. And for heaven's sake, think twice before you press that throttle.

CHAPTER 5

oh, so this is boot camp!

On November 28, 1965, the fighter plane of Howard Rutledge exploded under enemy fire. He parachuted into the hands of the North Vietnamese Army and was promptly placed in the "Heartbreak Hotel," one of the prisons in Hanoi.

When the door slammed and the key turned in that rusty, iron lock, a feeling of utter loneliness swept over me. I lay down on that cold cement slab in my 6 x 6 prison. The smell of human excrement burned my nostrils. A rat, large as a small cat, scampered across the slab beside me. The walls and floors and ceilings were caked with filth. Bars covered a tiny window high above the door. I was cold and hungry; my body ached from the swollen joints and sprained muscles . . .

It's hard to describe what solitary confinement can do to unnerve and defeat a man. You quickly tire of standing up or sitting down, sleeping or being awake. There are no books, no paper or pencils, no magazines or newspapers. The only colors you see are drab gray and dirty brown. Months or years may go by when you don't see the sunrise or the moon, green grass or flowers. You are locked in, alone and silent in your filthy little cell breathing stale, rotten air and trying to keep your sanity.[1]

Few of us will ever face the austere conditions of a POW camp. Yet to one degree or another, we all spend time behind bars.

- My e-mail today contains a prayer request for a young mother just diagnosed with lupus. Incarcerated by bad health.
- I had coffee yesterday with a man whose wife battles depression. He feels stuck (chain number one) and guilty for feeling stuck (chain number two).
- After half a century of marriage, a friend's wife began to lose her memory. He had to take away her car keys so she wouldn't drive. He has to stay near so she won't fall. They had hopes of growing old together. They still may, but only one of them will know the day of the week.

Each of these individuals wonders, *Where is heaven in this story? Why would God permit such imprisonment? Does this struggle serve any purpose?* Joseph surely posed those questions.

If Mrs. Potiphar couldn't flirt Joseph into her bed, she would force him. She grabbed for his robe, and he let her have it. He chose his character over his coat. When he ran, she concocted a story. When Potiphar came home, she was ready with her lie and Joseph's coat as proof. Potiphar charged Joseph with sexual assault and locked him in jail. "And [Joseph] was there in the prison. But the LORD was with Joseph and showed him mercy, and He gave him favor in the sight of the keeper of the prison" (Gen. 39:20–21).

Not a prison in the modern sense but a warren of underground, windowless rooms with damp floors, stale food, and bitter water. Guards shoved him into the dungeon and slammed the door. Joseph leaned back against the wall, slid to the floor. "I have done nothing here that they should put me into the dungeon" (40:15).

Joseph had done his best in Potiphar's house. He had made a fortune for his employer. He had kept his chores done and his room tidy. He had adapted to a new culture. He had resisted the sexual advances. But how was he rewarded? A prison sentence with no hope of parole. Since when does the high road lead over a cliff?

The answer? Ever since the events of Genesis 3, the chapter that documents the entry of evil into the world. Disaster came in the form of Lucifer, the fallen angel. And as long as Satan "prowls around like a roaring lion" (1 Peter 5:8 NIV), he will wreak havoc among God's people. He will lock preachers, like Paul, in prisons. He will exile pastors, like John, on remote islands. He will afflict the friends of Jesus, like Lazarus, with diseases. But his strategies always backfire. The imprisoned Paul wrote epistles. The banished John saw heaven. The cemetery of Lazarus became a stage upon which Christ performed one of his greatest miracles.

Intended evil becomes ultimate good.

As I reread that promise, it sounds formulaic, catchy, as if destined for a bumper sticker. I don't mean for it to. There is nothing trite about your wheelchair, empty pantry, or aching heart. These are uphill, into-the-wind challenges you are facing. They are not easy.

But neither are they random. God is not *sometimes* sovereign. He is not *occasionally* victorious. He does not occupy the throne one day and vacate it the next. "The Lord shall not turn back until He has executed and accomplished the thoughts and intents of His mind" (Jer. 30:24 AMP). This season in which you find yourself may puzzle you, but it does not bewilder God. He can and will use it for his purpose.

Case in point: Joseph in prison. From an earthly viewpoint the Egyptian jail was the tragic conclusion of Joseph's life. Satan could chalk up a victory for the dark side. All plans to use Joseph ended with the slamming of the jail door. The devil had Joseph just where he wanted him.

So did God.

> There in prison, they bruised [Joseph's] feet with fetters
>> and placed his neck in an iron collar.
> Until the time came to fulfill his word,
>> the LORD *tested* Joseph's character. (Ps. 105:18–19 NLT)[2]

What Satan intended for evil, God used for testing. In the Bible a test is an external trial that purifies and prepares the heart. Just as a fire refines precious metal from dross and impurities, a trial purges the heart of the same. One of the psalmists wrote:

> For you, O God, tested us;
>> you refined us like silver.
> You brought us into prison
>> and laid burdens on our backs.
> You let men ride over our heads;
>> we went through fire and water,
>> but you brought us to a place of abundance.
> (Ps. 66:10–12 NIV)

Every day God tests us through people, pain, or problems. Stop and consider your circumstances. Can you identify the tests of today? Snarling traffic? Threatening weather? Aching joints?

If you see your troubles as nothing more than isolated hassles and hurts, you'll grow bitter and angry. Yet if you see your troubles as tests used by God for his glory and your maturity, then even the smallest incidents take on significance.

A couple of days ago my Saturday afternoon turned into a tough test. Denalyn and I had a disagreement. We had agreed to sell our house, but we couldn't agree on a Realtor. I had my opinion, and she had hers. Back and forth we went, neither able to convince the other. A pleasant day turned sour. She retreated into her corner and I into mine.

We have Saturday worship services at our church. When the time came for me to leave and preach, I gave Denalyn a perfunctory *good-bye* and walked out the door to do God's work. "We'll deal with this later," I told her.

But God wanted to deal with me immediately. The distance between my house and the church building is only a five-minute drive. But that is all it took for God to prick my conscience with the truth. *Shouldn't you be at peace with your wife before you preach to my church?*

It was a test. Would I pout or apologize? Would I ignore the tension or deal with it? I can't say I always pass the tests, but that day I did with flying colors. Before the service began, I called Denalyn, apologized for my stubbornness, and asked for her forgiveness. Later that night we reached a decision on a Realtor, prayed together, and put the matter to rest.

Each day has a pop quiz. And some seasons are final exams. Brutal, sudden pitfalls of stress, sickness, or sadness. Like Joseph, you did your best. Like Joseph, your best was rewarded with incarceration. What is the purpose of the test? Why didn't God keep Joseph out of prison? Might this be the answer? "For when your faith is tested, your endurance has a chance to grow. So let it grow, for when your endurance is fully developed, you will be strong in character and ready for anything" (James 1:3–4 NLT).

As a boy Joseph was prone to softness. Jacob indulged him, spoiled him. Joseph talked about his dreams and grand ambitions. A bit too full of himself, perhaps. Even in Potiphar's house Joseph was the darling of the estate. Quickly promoted, often noticed. Success came easily. Perhaps pride did as well. If so, a prison term would purge that. God knew the challenges that lay ahead, and he used Joseph's time in prison to strengthen his servant.

"And the keeper of the prison committed to Joseph's hand all the prisoners who were in the prison; whatever they did there, it was his doing" (Gen. 39:22). Talk about a crash course in leadership! Joseph managed willing servants for Potiphar. But in prison he was assigned unruly, disrespectful, and ungrateful men. Joseph could have cloistered himself in a corner and mumbled, "I've learned my lesson. I'm not running anything for anybody." But he didn't complain, didn't criticize. He displayed a willing spirit with the prisoners.

He was especially kind to a butler and a baker. The butler and the baker, both officers of Pharaoh, were placed in Joseph's care. One morning he noticed deep frowns on their faces. He could have dismissed their expressions. What concern was their sorrow to him? Who cared if they were sullen or bitter? Joseph, however, took an interest in them. In fact, the first recorded words of Joseph in the prison were kind ones: "Why do you look so sad?" (40:7). Abandoned by his brothers, sold into slavery, and unjustly imprisoned, Joseph was still tender toward others. Wouldn't compassion be a suitable quality for the soon-to-be director of a worldwide hunger-relief program?

God wasn't finished. Both the baker and the butler were troubled by dreams. In his dream the butler saw a vine with three grape-bearing branches. He pressed the grapes into Pharaoh's cup and gave it to the king. The baker dreamed about bread. Three baskets were on his head, and birds ate the bread in the top basket. Both men sought the counsel of Joseph. And Joseph received an interpretation from God. Would he share it? The last time Joseph spoke of dreams, he ended up in a dry cistern. Besides, only 50 percent of his revelation was good news. Could Joseph be trusted to share God's news? If called to stand before Pharaoh, would Joseph accurately convey God's word? This was a test. Joseph passed it. He gave the butler good news ("You'll be out in three days") and the baker bad news ("You'll be dead in three days"). One would get a new start; the other, a noose around the neck.

Test, test, test. The dungeon looked like a prison, smelled like a prison, sounded like a prison, but had you asked the angels of heaven about Joseph's location, they would have replied, "Oh, he is in boot camp."

This chapter in your life looks like rehab, smells like unemployment, sounds like a hospital, but ask the angels. "Oh, she is in training."

God hasn't forgotten you. Just the opposite. He has chosen to train you. The Hebrew verb for *test* comes from a word that means "to take a keen look at, to look, to choose."[3] Dismiss the notion that God does not see your struggle. On the contrary, God is fully engaged. He sees the needs of tomorrow and, accordingly, uses your circumstances to create the test of today.

Does he not have the authority to do so? He is the Potter; we are the clay. He is the Shepherd; we are the sheep. He is the Gardener; we are the branches. He is the Teacher; we are the students. Trust his training. You'll get through this. If God can make a prince out of a prisoner, don't you think he can make something good out of your mess?

Remember, all tests are temporary. They are limited in duration. "In this you greatly rejoice, though now *for a little while* you may have had to suffer grief in all kinds of trials" (1 Peter 1:6 NIV).[4] Tests never last forever because this life doesn't last forever. "We were born but yesterday . . . Our days on earth are as transient as a shadow" (Job 8:9 NLT). Some tests end on earth, but all tests will end in heaven.

In the meantime, follow the example of Joseph. Let God train you. He is watching the way you handle the little jobs. If you are faithful with a few matters, he will set you over many (Matt. 25:21). Joseph succeeded in the kitchen and dungeon before he succeeded in the court. He cared for the butler and baker before he cared for the nations. The reward of good work is greater work. Do you aspire to great things? Excel in the small things. Show up on time. Finish your work early. Don't complain. Let others grumble in the corner of the prison cell. Not you. You know how God shapes his servants. Today's prisoner may become tomorrow's prime minister. When you are given a task, take it on.

When you see a hurt, address it. What if Joseph had ignored the sadness on the faces of Pharaoh's officers? What if he had focused on his needs and ignored theirs? Would God still have liberated him from prison? We don't know. But we know this: the kindness of Joseph opened the door of the jail because the cupbearer introduced Joseph to Pharaoh. Compassion matters to God. This is the time for service, not self-centeredness. Cancel the pity party. Love the people God brings to you.

And share the message God gives to you. This test will become your testimony. "[God] comes alongside us when we go through hard times, and before you know it, he brings us alongside someone else who is going through hard times so that we can be there for that person just as God was there for us" (2 Cor. 1:4 MSG).

You didn't sign up for this crash course in single parenting or caring for a disabled spouse, did you? No, God enrolled you. He has taken the intended evil and rewoven it into his curriculum. Why? So you can teach others what he has taught you. Your mess can become your message.

I like the conversation Bob Benson recounts in his book *"See You at the House."* One of his friends had a heart attack. Although, at first, the friend wasn't sure he'd survive, he did recover. Months after the surgery Bob asked him:

"Well, how did you like your heart attack?"

"It scared me to death, almost."

"Would you like to do it again?"

"No!"

"Would you recommend it?"

"Definitely not."

"Does your life mean more to you now than it did before?"

"Well, yes."

"You and Nell have always had a beautiful marriage, but are you closer now than ever?"

"Yes."

"How about that new granddaughter?"

"Yes. Did I show you her picture?"

"Do you have a new compassion for people—a deeper understanding and sympathy?"

"Yes."

"Do you know the Lord in a deeper, richer fellowship than you had ever realized could be possible?"

"Yes."

" . . . how'd you like your heart attack?"[5]

Rather than say, "God, why?" ask, "God, what?" *What* can I learn from this experience? "Remember today what you have learned about the LORD through your experiences with him" (Deut. 11:2 TEV). Rather than ask God to change your circumstances, ask him to use your circumstances to change you. Life is a required course. Might as well do your best to pass it.

God is at work in each of us whether we know it or not, whether we want it or not. "He takes no pleasure in making life hard, in throwing roadblocks in the way" (Lam. 3:33 MSG). He does not relish our sufferings, but he delights in our development. "God began doing a good work in you, and I am sure he will continue it until it is finished when Jesus Christ comes again" (Phil. 1:6 NCV). He will not fail. He cannot fail. He will "work in us what is pleasing to him" (Heb. 13:21 NIV). Every challenge, large or small, can equip you for a future opportunity.

Howard Rutledge came to appreciate his time as a POW in Vietnam. He wrote:

> During those long periods of enforced reflection, it became so much easier to separate the important from the trivial, the worth-while from the waste . . .
>
> My hunger for spiritual food soon outdid my hunger for a steak . . . I wanted to know about the part of me that will never die . . . I wanted to talk about God and Christ and the church . . . It took prison to show me how empty life is without God . . .
>
> On August 31, after twenty-eight days of torture, I could remember I had children but not how many. I said Phyllis's name over and over again so I would not forget. I prayed for strength. It was on that twenty-eighth night I made God a promise. If I survived this ordeal, the first Sunday back in freedom I would take Phyllis and my family to their church and . . . confess my faith in Christ

and join the church. This wasn't a deal with God to get me through that last miserable night. It was a promise made after months of thought. It took prison and hours of painful reflection to realize how much I needed God and the community of believers. After I made God that promise, again I prayed for strength to make it through the night.

When the morning dawned through the crack in the bottom of that solid prison door, I thanked God for His mercy.[6]

Don't see your struggle as an interruption to life but as preparation for life. No one said the road would be easy or painless. But God will use this mess for something good. "This trouble you're in isn't punishment; it's *training*, the normal experience of children . . . God is doing what *is* best for us, training us to live God's holy best" (Heb. 12:8, 10 MSG).

wait while God works

So here I sit in the waiting room. The receptionist took my name, recorded my insurance data, and gestured to a chair. "Please have a seat. We will call you when the doctor is ready." I look around. A mother holds a sleeping baby. A fellow dressed in a suit thumbs through *Time* magazine. A woman with a newspaper looks at her watch, sighs, and continues the task of the hour: waiting.

The waiting room. Not the examination room. That's down the hall. Not the consultation room. That's on the other side of the wall. Not the treatment room. Exams, consultations, and treatments all come later.

The task at hand is the name of the room: the waiting room. We in the waiting room understand our assignment: to wait. We don't treat each other. I don't ask the nurse for a stethoscope or blood pressure cuff. I don't pull up a chair next to the woman with the newspaper and say, "Tell me what prescriptions you are taking." That's the job of the nurse. My job is to wait. So I do.

Can't say that I like it. Time moves like an Alaskan glacier. The clock ticks every five minutes, not every second. Someone pressed the pause button. Life in slo-mo. We don't like to wait. We are the giddyup generation. We weave through traffic, looking for the faster lane. We frown at the person who takes eleven items into the ten-item express checkout. We drum our fingers while the song downloads or the microwave heats our coffee. "Come on, come on." We want six-pack abs in ten minutes and minute rice in thirty seconds. We don't like to wait. Not on the doctor, the traffic, or the pizza.

Not on God?

Take a moment and look around you. Do you realize where we sit? This planet is God's waiting room.

The young couple in the corner? Waiting to get pregnant. The fellow with the briefcase? He has résumés all over the country, waiting on work. The elderly woman with the cane? A widow. Been waiting a year for one tearless day. Waiting. Waiting on God to give, help, heal. Waiting on God to come. We indwell the land betwixt prayer offered and prayer answered. The land of waiting.

If anyone knew the furniture of God's waiting room, Joseph did. One problem with reading his story is its brevity. We can read the Genesis account from start to finish in less than an hour, which gives the impression that all these challenges took place before breakfast one morning. We'd be wiser to pace our reading over a couple of decades.

Take chapter 37 into a dry cistern, and sit there for a couple of hours while the sun beats down. Recite the first verse of chapter 39 over and over for a couple of months: "Now Joseph had been taken down to Egypt." Joseph needed at least this much time to walk the 750 miles from Dothan to Thebes.

Then there was the day or days or weeks on the auction block. Add to that probably a decade in Potiphar's house, supervising the servants, doing his master's bidding, learning Egyptian. Ticktock. Ticktock. Ticktock. Time moves slowly in a foreign land.

And time stands still in a prison.

Joseph had asked the butler to put in a good word for him. "Remember me when it is well with you, and please show kindness to me; make mention of me to Pharaoh, and get me out of this house . . . I have done nothing here that they should put me into the dungeon" (Gen. 40:14–15).

We can almost hear the butler reply, "Certainly, I will mention you to Pharaoh. First chance I get. You'll be hearing from me." Joseph hurried back to his cell and collected his belongings. He wanted to be ready when the call came. A day passed. Then two. Then a week . . . a month. Six months. No word. As it turned out, "Pharaoh's cup-bearer . . . promptly forgot all about Joseph, never giving him another thought" (v. 23 NLT).

On the page of your Bible, the uninked space between that verse and the next is scarcely wider than a hair ribbon. It takes your eyes only a split second to see it. Yet it took Joseph two years to experience it. Chapter 41 starts like this: "Two years passed and Pharaoh had a dream" (v. 1 MSG).

Two years! Twenty-four months of silence. One hundred and four weeks of waiting. Seven hundred and thirty days of wondering. Two thousand one hundred and ninety meals alone. Seventeen thousand five hundred and twenty hours of listening for God yet hearing nothing but silence.

Plenty of time to grow bitter, cynical, angry. Folks have given up on God for lesser reasons in shorter times.

Not Joseph. On a day that began like any other, he heard a stirring at the dungeon entrance. Loud, impatient voices demanded, "We are here for the Hebrew! Pharaoh wants the Hebrew!" Joseph looked up from his corner to see the prison master, white-faced and stammering. "Get up! Hurry, get up!" Two guards from the court were on his heels. Joseph remembered them from his days in Potiphar's service. They took him by the elbows and marched him out of the hole. He squinted at the brilliant sunlight. They walked him across a courtyard into a room. Attendants flocked around him. They removed his soiled clothing, washed his body, and shaved his beard. They dressed him in a white robe and new sandals. The guards reappeared and walked him into the throne room.

And so it was that Joseph and Pharaoh looked into each other's eyes for the first time.

The king hadn't slept well the night before. Dreams troubled his rest. He heard of Joseph's skill. "They say you can interpret dreams. My counselors are mute as stones. Can you help me?"

Joseph's last two encounters hadn't ended so well. Mrs. Potiphar lied about him. The butler forgot about him. In both cases Joseph had mentioned the name of God. Perhaps he should hedge his bets and keep his faith under wraps.

He didn't. "Not I, but God. God will set Pharaoh's mind at ease" (v. 16 MSG).

Joseph emerged from his prison cell bragging on God. Jail time didn't devastate his faith; it deepened it.

And you? You aren't in prison, but you may be *in*fertile or *in*active or *in* limbo or *in* between jobs or *in* search of health, help, a house, or a spouse. Are you in God's waiting room? If so, here is what you need to know: *while you wait, God works.*

"My Father is always at his work," Jesus said (John 5:17 NIV). God never twiddles his thumbs. He never stops. He takes no vacations. He rested on the seventh day of creation but got back to work on the eighth and hasn't stopped since. Just because you are idle, don't assume God is.

Joseph's story appeared to stall out in chapter 40. Our hero was in shackles. The train was off the tracks. History was in a holding pattern. But while Joseph was waiting, God was working. He assembled the characters. God placed the butler in Joseph's care. He stirred the sleep of the king with odd dreams. He confused Pharaoh's counselors. And at just the right time, God called Joseph to duty.

He's working for you as well. "Be still, and know that I am God"[1] reads the sign on God's waiting room wall. You can be glad because

God is good. You can be still because he is active. You can rest because he is busy.

Remember God's word through Moses to the Israelites? "Do not be afraid. Stand still, and see the salvation of the LORD . . . The LORD will fight for you, and you shall hold your peace" (Ex. 14:13–14). The Israelites saw the Red Sea ahead of them and heard the Egyptian soldiers thundering after them. Death on both sides. *Stand still? Are you kidding?* But what the former slaves couldn't see was the hand of God at the bottom of the water, creating a path, and his breath from heaven, separating the waters. God was working for them.

God worked for Mary, the mother of Jesus. The angel told her that she would become pregnant. The announcement stirred a torrent of questions in her heart. How would she become pregnant? What would people think? What would Joseph say? Yet God was working for her. He sent a message to Joseph, her fiancé. God prompted Caesar to declare a census. God led the family to Bethlehem. "God is always at work for the good of everyone who loves him" (Rom. 8:28 CEV).

To wait, biblically speaking, is not to assume the worst, worry, fret, make demands, or take control. Nor is waiting inactivity. Waiting is a sustained effort to stay focused on God through prayer and belief. To wait is to "rest in the LORD, and wait patiently for Him; . . . not fret" (Ps. 37:7).

Nehemiah shows us how to do this. His book is a memoir of his efforts to reconstruct the walls of Jerusalem. His story starts with a date. "It happened in the month of Chislev, in the twentieth year, as I was in Susa the citadel, that Hanani . . . came with certain men from Judah" (Neh. 1:1–2 ESV). They brought bad news. Hostile forces had flattened the walls that had once guarded the city. Even the gates had been burned. The few remaining Jews were in "great trouble and shame" (v. 3 ESV).

Nehemiah responded with prayer. "O Lord, let your ear be attentive to the prayer of your servant . . . and give success to your servant today, and grant him mercy in the sight of this man" (v. 11 ESV).

"This man" was King Artaxerxes, the monarch of Persia. Nehemiah was his personal cupbearer, on call twenty-four hours a day, seven days a week. Nehemiah could not leave his post and go to Jerusalem. Even if he could, he had no resources with which to rebuild the walls. So he resolved to wait on the Lord in prayer.

The first verse of the second chapter reveals the length of his wait. "And it came to pass in the month of Nisan" that Nehemiah was appointed to a spot on the king's Jerusalem Commission. How far apart were the dates? Four months. Nehemiah's request, remember, was immediate: "Give your servant success today" (NIV). God answered the request four months (!) after Nehemiah made it.

Waiting is easier read than done. It doesn't come easily for me. I've been in a hurry my whole life. Hurrying to school, hurrying to finish homework. Pedal faster, drive quicker. I used to put my wristwatch face on the inside of my arm so I wouldn't lose the millisecond it took to turn my wrist. What insanity! I wonder if I could have obeyed God's ancient command to keep the Sabbath holy. To slow life to a crawl for twenty-four hours. The Sabbath was created for frantic souls like me, people who need this weekly reminder: the world will not stop if you do!

And what of this command: "Three times a year all your men are to appear before the Sovereign LORD, the God of Israel. I will drive out nations before you and enlarge your territory, and no one will covet your land when you go up three times each year to appear before the LORD your God" (Ex. 34:23–24 NIV)? God instructed the promised land settlers to stop their work three times a year and gather for worship. All commerce, education, government, and industry came to a halt while the people assembled. Can you imagine this happening today? Our country would be utterly defenseless.

Yet God promised to protect the territory. No one would encroach upon the Israelites. What's more, they wouldn't even desire to do so. "No one will covet your land." God used the pilgrimage to teach this principle: if you will wait in worship, I will work for you.

Daniel did this. In one of the most dramatic examples of waiting in the Bible, this Old Testament prophet kept his mind on God for an extended period. His people had been oppressed for almost seventy years. Daniel entered into a time of prayer on their behalf. For twenty-one days he abstained from pleasant food, meat, and wine. He labored in prayer. He persisted, pleaded, and agonized.

No response.

Then on the twenty-second day a breakthrough. An angel of God appeared. He revealed to Daniel the reason for the long delay. Daniel's prayer was heard on the first day it was offered. The angel was dispatched with a response. "That very day I was sent here to meet you. But for twenty-one days the mighty Evil Spirit who overrules the kingdom of Persia blocked my way. Then Michael, one of the top officers of the heavenly army, came to help me, so that I was able to break through these spirit rulers of Persia" (Dan. 10:12–13 TLB).

From an earthly perspective nothing was happening. Daniel's prayers were falling like pebbles on hard ground. But from a heavenly perspective a battle was raging in the heavens. Two angels were engaged in fierce combat for three weeks. While Daniel was waiting, God was working.

What if Daniel had given up? Lost faith? Walked away from God?

Better questions: What if you give up? Lose faith? Walk away?

Don't. For heaven's sake, don't. All of heaven is warring on your behalf. Above and around you at this very instant, God's messengers are at work.

Keep waiting.

> Those who wait on the LORD
> Shall renew their strength;
> They shall mount up with wings like eagles,
> They shall run and not be weary,
> They shall walk and not faint. (Isa. 40:31)

Fresh strength. Renewed vigor. Legs that don't grow weary. Delight yourself in God, and he will bring rest to your soul.

You'll get through this waiting room season just fine. Pay careful note, and you will detect the most wonderful surprise. The doctor will step out of his office and take the seat next to yours. "Just thought I'd keep you company while you are waiting." Not every physician will do that, but yours will. After all, he is the Great Physician.

more bounce back than bozo

D on't hold me to the precise details of this childhood memory. I can't recall the name of the kid who had the party. Nor do I know my exact age, though judging from the neighborhood in which we were living, I must have been about eight years old. I don't remember the games we played or the names of the other guests. But I do remember the bounce-back clown.

He was pear-shaped, narrower at the top than the bottom. Inflated and Bozo-like. He was as tall as I was. All his facial features were painted on him. Ears didn't protrude. Nose didn't stick out. Even his arms lay flat. He didn't make music at the touch of a button or recite lines at the pull of a string. He didn't do anything except this: bounce back.

Knock him down; he popped right up. Clobber him with a bat, pop him in the nose, or give him a swift kick to the side, and he would fall down—but not for long.

We did our best to level the clown. One punch after the other, each more vicious than the prior hit. None of us succeeded. Bozo had more comeback than the '69 Mets. He wasn't strong; he was full of air. He couldn't duck or defend himself. He didn't charm us with good looks or silence attackers with quick wit. He was a clown, for goodness' sake. Red lips and yellow hair. Yet there was something about him, or within him, that kept him on his feet.

We'd do well to learn his secret. Life comes at us with a fury of flying fists—right hook of rejection, sucker punch of loss. Enemies hit below the belt. Calamities cause us to stagger. It's a slugfest out there.

Some people once knocked down never get up. They stay on the mat—beaten, bitter, broken. Out for the count. Others, however, have more bounce back than Bozo.

Joseph did. The guy was a walking piñata. The angry jealousy of his brothers that sold him into slavery, the below-the-belt deceit by Potiphar's wife that landed him in prison, the butler's broken promise that kept him in prison. Joseph staggered but recovered. (Cue *Rocky* music.) By God's strength, he pulled himself to his feet and stood, stronger than ever, in Pharaoh's court.

Pharaoh was the unrivaled ruler of the land. He was his own cabinet and congress. He spoke the word, and it was done. He issued a command, and it was law. He entered a room, and he was worshiped. Yet on this particular day Pharaoh didn't feel worshipworthy.

Let's imagine the prototypical Pharaoh: bare chested and rock jawed, saggy in the pecs, but solid for a middle-aged monarch. He wears a cloth on his shoulders and on his head a leather cone encircled by a rearing cobra. His beard is false, and his eye makeup is almond shaped. He holds a staff in one hand and rests his chin in the other. Slaves fan the air about him. A bowl of figs and nuts sits within arm's reach on a table. But he isn't hungry. He just frowns. His attendants speak in anxious, subdued voices. When Pharaoh isn't happy, no one is happy.

Dreams kept him up half the night. In dream number one, cows grazed on the riverbank. Seven were fine and fat, prime candidates for a Chick-fil-A commercial. But while the healthy bovines weren't looking, seven skinny cows sneaked up from behind and devoured them. Pharaoh sat up in bed and broke out in a sweat.

After a few minutes he dismissed the dream and fell back asleep. But dream number two was just as bothersome. A stalk of grain with seven healthy heads was consumed by a stalk of grain with seven withered heads. Two dreams with the same pattern: the seven bad devoured the seven good.

Pharaoh woke up distracted and befuddled. He assembled his council and demanded an interpretation. Cows consuming cows, stalks gobbling stalks. Did the dreams mean anything? His council had no response, had not a clue. His butler then remembered Joseph from their days together in prison. So the butler told Pharaoh about the Hebrew's skill at dream interpretation. The king snapped his finger, and a flourish of activity ensued. Joseph was cleaned up and called in. In a moment of high drama, Jacob's favored son was escorted into Pharaoh's throne room.

Oh, the contrast. Pharaoh, the king. Joseph, the ex-shepherd. Pharaoh, urban. Joseph, rural. Pharaoh from the palace. Joseph from the prison. Pharaoh wore gold chains. Joseph wore bruises from shackles. Pharaoh had his armies and pyramids. Joseph had a borrowed robe and a foreign accent.

The prisoner, however, was unfazed. He heard the dreams and went straight to work. No need to consult advisers or tea leaves. This was simple stuff, like basic multiplication for a Harvard math professor. "Expect seven years of plenty and seven years of famine." No one, including Pharaoh, knew how to respond. *Famine* was a foul word in the Egyptian dictionary. The nation didn't manufacture Chevys or export T-shirts. Their civilization was built on farms. Crops made Egypt the jewel of the Nile. Agriculture made Pharaoh the most powerful man in the world. A monthlong drought would hurt the economy. A yearlong famine would weaken the throne of Pharaoh, who owned the fields around the Nile. A seven-year famine would turn the Nile into a creek and the crops to sticks. A famine to Pharaoh was the equivalent of electric cars to the sheiks. Apocalypse!

The silence in the throne room was so thick you could hear a cough drop. Joseph took advantage of the pause in conversation to offer a solution. "Create a department of agriculture, and commission a smart person to gather grain in the good years and to distribute it during the lean years."

Officials gulped at Joseph's chutzpah. It was one thing to give bad news to Pharaoh, another to offer unsolicited advice. Yet the guy hadn't shown a hint of fear since he entered the palace. He paid no homage to the king. He didn't offer accolades to the magicians. He didn't kiss rings or polish apples. Lesser men would have cowered. Joseph didn't blink.

Again the contrast. The most powerful person in the room, Pharaoh (ruler of the Nile, deity of the heavens, Grand Pooh-Bah of the pyramid people), was in dire need of a scotch. The lowest person in the pecking order, Joseph (ex-slave, convict, accused sex offender), was cooler than the other side of the pillow.

What made the difference?

Ballast. Bozo had it. The clown at the birthday party, I came to learn, was braced by a lead weight. A three-pound plate hidden at his base served as a counterbalance against the punches. Joseph, as it turns out, had a similar anchor. Not a piece of iron but a deep-seated, stabilizing belief in God's sovereignty.

We sense it in his first sentence: "It is not in me; God will give Pharaoh . . ." (Gen. 41:16). The second time Joseph spoke, he explained, "God has shown Pharaoh what He is about to do" (v. 28). Joseph proceeded to interpret the dreams and then tell Pharaoh that the dreams were "established by God, and God will shortly bring it to pass" (v. 32).

Four times in three verses Joseph made reference to God! "God . . . God . . . God . . . God."

Haven't we seen this before? When Potiphar's wife attempted to seduce him, Joseph refused, saying, "How then could I do such a wicked thing and sin against God?" (Gen. 39:9 NIV). When fellow prisoners asked for an interpretation of their dreams, Joseph said, "Do not interpretations belong to God?" (40:8). He locked the magnet of his compass on a divine polestar. He lived with the awareness that God was active, able, and up to something significant.

And Joseph was correct. Pharaoh commanded a stunning turnaround: "Can we find such a one as this, a man in whom is the Spirit of God?" (41:38). He turned the kingdom over to Joseph. By the end of the day, the boy from Canaan was riding in a royal chariot, second only to Pharaoh in authority. What an unexpected rebound.

In the chaos called "Joseph's life," I count one broken promise, at least two betrayals, several bursts of hatred, two abductions, more than one attempted seduction, ten jealous brothers, and one case of poor parenting. Abuse. Unjust imprisonment. Twenty-four months of prison food. Mix it all together and let it sit for thirteen years, and what do you get? The grandest bounce back in the Bible! Jacob's forgotten boy became the second most powerful man in the world's most powerful country. The path to the palace wasn't quick, and it wasn't painless, but wouldn't you say that God took this mess and made it into something good?

And wouldn't you think he can do the same with yours? Tally up the pain of your past. Betrayals plus anger plus tragedies. Poorly parented? Wrongly accused? Inappropriately touched? Oh, how onerous life can be.

Yet consider this question: Is the God of Joseph still in control? Yes! Can he do for you what he did for Joseph? Yes! Might the evil intended to harm you actually help you become the person God intends you to be? Yes! Someday—perhaps in this life, certainly in the next—you will tally up the crud of your life and write this sum: all good.

Lieutenant Sam Brown did. Two years out of West Point, he was on his first tour of duty in Afghanistan when an improvised explosive device turned his Humvee into a Molotov cocktail. He doesn't remember how he got out of the truck. He does remember rolling in the sand, slapping dirt on his burning face, running in circles, and finally dropping to his knees. He lifted flaming arms to the air and cried, "Jesus, save me!"

In Sam's case the words were more than a desperate scream. He is a devoted believer in Jesus Christ. Sam was calling on his Savior to take him home. He assumed he would die.

But death did not come. His gunner did. With bullets flying around them, he helped Sam reach cover. Crouching behind a wall, Sam realized that bits of his clothing were fusing to his skin. He ordered the private to rip his gloves off the burning flesh. The soldier hesitated, then pulled. With the gloves came pieces of his hands. Brown winced at what was the first of thousands of moments of pain.

When vehicles from another platoon reached them, they loaded the wounded soldier into a truck. Before Sam passed out, he caught a glimpse of his singed face in the mirror. He didn't recognize himself.

That was September 2008. By the time I met him three years later, he had undergone dozens of painful surgeries. Dead skin had been excised and healthy skin harvested and grafted. The pain chart didn't have a number high enough to register the agony he felt.

Yet in the midst of the horror, beauty walked in. Dietitian Amy Larsen. Since Sam's mouth had been reduced to the size of a coin, Amy monitored his nutrition intake. He remembers the first time he saw her. Dark hair, brown eyes. Nervous. Cute. More important, she didn't flinch at the sight of him.

After several weeks he gathered the courage to ask her out. They went to a rodeo. The following weekend they went to a friend's wedding. During the three-hour drive Amy told Sam how she had noticed him months earlier when he was in ICU, covered with bandages, sedated with morphine, and attached to a breathing machine. When he regained consciousness, she stepped into his room to meet him. But there was a circle of family and doctors, so she turned and left.

The two continued to see each other. Early in their relationship Sam brought up the name Jesus Christ. Amy was not a believer. Sam's story stirred her heart for God. Sam talked to her about God's mercy and led her to Christ. Soon thereafter they were married. And as I write these words, they are the parents of a seven-month-old boy. Sam directs a program to aid wounded soldiers.[1]

Far be it from me to minimize the horror of a man on fire in the Afghan desert. And who can imagine the torture of repeated surgeries and rehab? The emotional stress has taken its toll on their marriage at times. Yet Sam and Amy have come to believe this: God's math works differently than ours. *War + near death + agonizing rehab = wonderful family and hope for a bright future.* In God's hand intended evil is eventual good.

With God's help you can bounce back. Who knows? Your rebound may happen today. On the morning of his promotion, Joseph had no reason to think the day would be different from the seven hundred prior ones. I doubt that he prayed, *God, please promote me to prime minister of Egypt before sunset.* But God exceeded Joseph's fondest prayer. Joseph began the day in prison and ended it in a palace. As he dozed off to sleep, he is reported to have smiled to himself and whispered, "Just as Max said, I have more bounce back than Bozo."

CHAPTER 8

is God good when life isn't?

I remember the day as a sunny, summer Brazilian one. Denalyn and I were spending the afternoon with our friends Paul and Debbie. Their house was a welcome respite. We lived close to downtown Rio de Janeiro in a high-rise apartment. Paul and Debbie lived an hour away from the city center in a nice house where the air was cooler, the streets were cleaner, and life was calmer. Besides, they had a swimming pool.

Our two-year-old daughter, Jenna, loved to play with their kids. And that is exactly what she was doing when she fell. We didn't intend to leave the children unattended. We had stepped into the house for just a moment to fill our plates. We were chatting and chewing when Paul and Debbie's four-year-old walked into the room and casually told her mom, "Jenna fell in the pool." We exploded out the door. Jenna was flopping in the water, wearing neither floaties nor a life jacket. Paul reached her first. He jumped in and lifted her up to Denalyn. Jenna coughed and cried for a minute, and just like that she was fine. Tragedy averted. Daughter safe.

Imagine our gratitude. We immediately circled up the kids, offered a prayer, and sang a song of thanks. For the remainder of the day, our feet didn't touch the ground, and Jenna didn't leave our arms. Even driving home, I was thanking God. In the rearview mirror I could see Jenna sound asleep in her car seat, and I offered yet another prayer: *God, you are so good.* Then a question surfaced in my thoughts.

From God? Or from the part of me that struggles to make sense out of God? I can't say. But what the voice asked, I still remember: *If Jenna hadn't survived, would God still be good?*

I had spent the better part of the afternoon broadcasting God's goodness. Yet had we lost Jenna, would I have reached a different verdict? Is God good only when the outcome is?

When the cancer is in remission, we say "God is good." When the pay raise comes, we announce "God is good." When the university admits us or the final score favors our team, "God is good." Would we and do we say the same under different circumstances? In the cemetery as well as the nursery? In the unemployment line as well as the grocery line? In days of recession as much as in days of provision? Is God always good?

For my friends Brian and Christyn Taylor, the question is more than academic. During this last year their seven-year-old daughter was hospitalized for more than six months with six surgeries for a disease of the pancreas, Brian's job was discontinued, several family members died and another was diagnosed with brain cancer, and Christyn was pregnant with child number four. Life was tough. She blogged:

> Multiple hospital stays with my daughter were exhausting, but I held faith. Losing Brian's family members one by one until there was only one left, who was then diagnosed with stage 4 brain cancer, was incomprehensible, but I still held faith. Being hospitalized seven-and-a-half weeks with a placental abruption was terrifying, but I held faith. I held to the faith that God works for my good, and though I did not necessarily understand the trials, I trusted God's bigger, unseen plan.
>
> God and I had a deal—I would endure the trials that came my way as long as he acknowledged my stopping point. He knew where

my line had been drawn, and I knew in my heart he would never cross it.

He did. I delivered a stillborn baby girl. With my daughter Rebecca still at home on a feeding tube and her future health completely unknown, it was a foregone conclusion that this baby we so wanted and loved would be saved. She wasn't. My line in the sand was crossed. My one-way deal with God was shattered.

Everything changed in that moment. Fear set in, and my faith began to crumble. My "safety zone" with God was no longer safe. If this could happen in the midst of our greatest struggles, then anything was fair game. For the first time in my life, anxiety began to overwhelm me.[1]

We can relate. Most, if not all of us, have a contractual agreement with God. The fact that he hasn't signed it doesn't keep us from believing it.

I pledge to be a good, decent person, and in return God will . . .
    save my child.
    heal my wife.
    protect my job.
    (fill in the blank) _____.

Only fair, right? Yet when God fails to meet our bottom-line expectations, we are left spinning in a tornado of questions. Is he good at all? Is God angry at me? Stumped? Overworked? Is his power limited? His authority restricted? Did the devil outwit him? When life isn't good, what are we to think about God? Where is he in all this?

Joseph's words for Pharaoh offer some help here. We don't typically think of Joseph as a theologian. Not like Job, the sufferer, or

Paul, the apostle. For one thing we don't have many of Joseph's words. Yet the few we have reveal a man who wrestled with the nature of God.

To the king he announced:

> But afterward there will be seven years of famine so great that all the prosperity will be forgotten and wiped out. Famine will destroy the land. This famine will be so terrible that even the memory of the good years will be erased. As for having the dream twice, it means that the matter has been decreed by God and that he will make these events happen soon. (Gen. 41:30–32 NLT)

Joseph saw both seasons, the one of plenty and the one of paucity, beneath the umbrella of God's jurisdiction. Both were "decreed by God."

How could this be? Was the calamity God's idea?

Of course not. God never creates or parlays evil. "God can never do wrong! It is impossible for the Almighty to do evil" (Job 34:10 NCV; see also James 1:17). He is the essence of good. How can he who is good invent anything bad?

And he is sovereign. Scripture repeatedly attributes utter and absolute control to his hand. "The Most High God rules the kingdom of mankind and sets over it whom he will" (Dan. 5:21 ESV). God is good. God is sovereign. Then how are we to factor in the presence of calamities in God's world?

Here is how the Bible does it: God permits it. When the demons begged Jesus to send them into a herd of pigs, he "gave them permission" (Mark 5:12–13). Regarding the rebellious, God said, "I let them become defiled . . . that I might fill them with horror so they would know that I am the LORD" (Ezek. 20:26 NIV). The Old Law speaks of the consequence of accidentally killing a person: "If [the man] does not do it intentionally, but God lets it happen, he is to flee to a place I will designate" (Ex. 21:13 NIV).

God at times permits tragedies. He permits the ground to grow dry and stalks to grow bare. He allows Satan to unleash mayhem. But he doesn't allow Satan to triumph. Isn't this the promise of Romans 8:28: "And we know that in all things God works for the good of those who love him, who have been called according to his purpose" (NIV)? God promises to render beauty out of "all things," not "each thing." The isolated events may be evil, but the ultimate culmination is good.

We see small examples of this in our own lives. When you sip on a cup of coffee and say, "This is good," what are you saying? The plastic bag that contains the beans is good? The beans themselves are good? Hot water is good? A coffee filter is good? No, none of these. *Good* happens when the ingredients work together: the bag opened, the beans ground into powder, the water heated to the right temperature. It is the collective cooperation of the elements that creates good.

Nothing in the Bible would cause us to call a famine good or a heart attack good or a terrorist attack good. These are terrible calamities, born out of a fallen earth. Yet every message in the Bible, especially the story of Joseph, compels us to believe that God will mix them with other ingredients and bring good out of them.

But we must let God define *good*. Our definition includes health, comfort, and recognition. His definition? In the case of his Son, Jesus Christ, the good life consisted of struggles, storms, and death. But God worked it all together for the greatest of good: his glory and our salvation.

Joni Eareckson Tada has spent most of her life attempting to reconcile the presence of suffering with the nature of God. She was just a teenager when a diving accident left her paralyzed from the neck down. After more than forty years in a wheelchair, Joni has reached this conclusion:

> [Initially] I figured that if Satan and God were involved in my accident at all, then it must be that the devil had twisted God's arm for permission . . .
>
> I reasoned that once God granted permission to Satan, he then nervously had to run behind him with a repair kit, patching up what Satan had ruined, mumbling to himself, "Oh great, now how am I going to work this for good?" . . .
>
> But the truth is that God is infinitely more powerful than Satan . . .
>
> While the devil's motive in my disability was to shipwreck my faith by throwing a wheelchair in my way, I'm convinced that God's motive was to thwart the devil and use the wheelchair to change me and make me more like Christ through it all . . .
>
> [He can] bring ultimate good out of the devil's wickedness.[2]

This was the message of Jesus. When his followers spotted a blind man on the side of the road, they asked Jesus for an explanation. Was God angry? Who was to blame? Who sinned? Jesus' answer provided a higher option: the man was blind so "the works of God should be revealed in him" (John 9:3). God turned blindness, a bad thing, into a billboard for Jesus' power to heal. Satan acted, God counteracted, and good won. It's a divine jujitsu of sorts. God redirects the energy of evil against its source. "[God] uses evil to bring evil to nought."[3] He is the master chess player, always checkmating the devil's moves.

Our choice comes down to this: trust God or turn away. He will cross the line. He will shatter our expectations. And we will be left to make a decision.

Christyn Taylor made hers. Remember the young mother I told you about? She concluded her blog with these words:

> I have spent weeks trying to figure out why a God I so love could let this happen to my family at such a time. The only conclusion I came to was this: I have to give up my line in the sand. I have to offer my entire life, every minute portion of it, to God's control regardless of the outcome.
>
> My family is in God's hands. No lines have been drawn, no deals made. I have given our lives to the Lord. Peace has entered where panic once resided, and calmness settled where anxiety once ruled.[4]

At some point we all stand at this intersection. Is God good when the outcome is not? During the famine as well as the feast? The definitive answer comes in the person of Jesus Christ. He is the only picture of God ever taken. Do you want to know heaven's clearest answer to the question of suffering? Look at Jesus.

He pressed his fingers into the sore of the leper. He felt the tears of the sinful woman who wept. He inclined his ear to the cry of the hungry. He wept at the death of a friend. He stopped his work to tend to the needs of a grieving mother. He doesn't recoil, run, or retreat at the sight of pain. Just the opposite. He didn't walk the earth in an insulated bubble or preach from an isolated, germfree, pain-free island. He took his own medicine. He played by his own rules. Trivial irritations of family life? Jesus felt them. Cruel accusations of jealous men? Jesus knew their sting. A seemingly senseless death? Just look at the cross. He exacts nothing from us that he did not experience himself.

Why? Because he is good.

God owes us no more explanation than this. Besides, if he gave one, what makes us think we would understand it? Might the problem be less God's plan and more our limited perspective? Suppose the wife of George Frideric Handel came upon a page of her husband's famous oratorio *Messiah*. The entire work was more than two hundred pages long. Imagine that she discovered one page on the kitchen table. On it her husband had written only one measure in a minor key, one that didn't work on its own. Suppose she, armed with this fragment of dissonance, marched into his studio and said, "This music makes no sense. You are a lousy composer." What would he think?

Perhaps something similar to what God thinks when we do the same. We point to our minor key—our sick child, crutches, or famine—and say, "This makes no sense!" Yet out of all his creation, how much have we seen? And of all his work how much do we understand? Only a sliver. A doorway peephole. Is it possible that some explanation for suffering exists of which we know nothing at all? What if God's answer to the question of suffering requires more megabytes than our puny minds have been given?

And is it possible that the wonder of heaven will make the most difficult life a good bargain? This was Paul's opinion. "Our light and momentary troubles are achieving for us an eternal glory that far outweighs them all" (2 Cor. 4:17 NIV).

Suppose I invited you to experience the day of your dreams. Twenty-four hours on an island paradise with your favorite people, food, and activities. The only stipulation: one millisecond of discomfort. For reasons I choose not to explain, you will need to begin the day with the millisecond of distress.

Would you accept my offer? I think you would. A split second is nothing compared to twenty-four hours. On God's clock you're in the middle of your millisecond. Compared to eternity, what is seventy, eighty, ninety years? Just a vapor. Just a finger snap compared to heaven.

Your pain won't last forever, but you will. "Whatever we may have to go through now is less than nothing compared with the magnificent future God has in store for us" (Rom. 8:18 PHILLIPS).

What is coming will make sense of what is happening now. Let God finish his work. Let the composer complete his symphony. The forecast is simple. Good days. Bad days. But God is in *all* days. He is the Lord of the famine and the feast, and he uses both to accomplish his will.

a splash of gratitude with that attitude, please

Try as I might to seem cultured, my blue collar often peeks through my tux. It certainly did some years back when I was invited to a minister's house for tea. I was brand-new to ministry and to our city. He was a seasoned pastor from New Zealand, educated in England. When he asked me to speak at his church, I was honored. When he requested that I come to his house for tea, I was intrigued.

I had never heard of high tea. High fives and "hi, y'all!" and "hi-yippie-yi-yo-ki-yay," yes. But never high tea. Tea (to West Texas boys) means pitchers, tall glasses, ice cubes, and Lipton. In the spirit of adventure I gladly accepted the invitation. I even acted enthused at the sight of the tea and cookie tray. But then came the moment of truth. The hostess asked what I would like in my tea. She offered two options: "Lemon? Milk?" I had no clue, but I didn't want to be rude, and I sure didn't want to miss out on anything, so I said, "Both."

The look on her face left no doubt. I'd goofed. "You don't mix lemon and milk in the same cup," she softly explained, "unless you want a cup of curdle."

Some things were not made to coexist. Long-tailed cats and rocking chairs? Bad combination. Bulls in a china closet? Not a good idea. Blessings and bitterness? That mixture doesn't go over well with God. Combine heavenly kindness with earthly ingratitude and expect a sour concoction.

Perhaps you've sampled it. Gratitude doesn't come naturally. Self-pity does. Bellyaches do. Grumbles and mumbles—no one has to remind us to offer them. Yet they don't mix well with the kindness we have been given. A spoonful of gratitude is all we need.

Joseph took more than a spoonful. He had cause to be ungrateful. Abandoned. Enslaved. Betrayed. Estranged. Yet try as we might to find tinges of bitterness, we don't succeed. What we do discover, however, are two dramatic gestures of gratitude.

> And to Joseph were born two sons before the years of famine came, whom Asenath, the daughter of Poti-Pherah priest of On, bore to him. Joseph called the name of the firstborn Manasseh: "For God has made me forget all my toil and all my father's house." And the name of the second he called Ephraim: "For God has caused me to be fruitful in the land of my affliction." (Gen. 41:50–52)

Child naming is no small responsibility. The name sticks for life. Wherever the child goes, whenever the child is introduced, the parents' decision will be remembered. (Exactly what was Texas Governor Jim Hogg thinking when he named his daughter Ima?) Most parents go to great effort to select the perfect name for their children. Joseph did.

These were the days of abundance. God had rewarded Joseph with a place in Pharaoh's court and a wife for his own home. The time had come to start a family. The young couple was reclining on the couch when he reached over and patted Asenath's round, pregnant tummy. "I've been thinking about names for our baby."

"Oh, Joey, how sweet. I have as well. In fact, I bought a name-your-baby book at the grocery store."

"You won't need it. I already have the name."

"What is it?"

"God Made Me Forget."

"If he made you forget, how can you name him?"

"No, that is the name: God Made Me Forget."

She gave him that look Egyptian wives always gave their Hebrew husbands. "God Made Me Forget? Every time I call my son, I will say, 'God Made Me Forget'?" She shook her head and tried it out. "'It's time for dinner, God Made Me Forget. Come in and wash your hands, God Made Me Forget.' I don't know, Joseph. I was thinking something more like Tut or Ramses, or have you ever considered the name Max? It is a name reserved for special people."

"No, Asenath, my mind is made up. Each time my son's name is spoken, God's name will be praised. God made me forget all the pain and hurt I experienced at the hands of my brothers, and I want everyone to know—I want God to know—I am grateful."

Apparently Mrs. Joseph warmed to the idea because at the birth of son number two, she and Joseph called him God Made Me Fruitful. One name honored God's mercy; the other proclaimed his favor.

Do you think God noticed Joseph's gesture? A New Testament story provides an answer. Many centuries later "Jesus . . . reached the border between Galilee and Samaria. As he entered a village there, ten lepers stood at a distance, crying out, 'Jesus, Master, have mercy on us!'" (Luke 17:11–13 NLT).

Maybe the men awaited Jesus as he turned a bend in the path. Or perhaps they appeared from behind a grove of trees or a cluster of rocks. Though we don't know how they came, we can be sure what they yelled. "Unclean! Unclean!" The warning was unnecessary. Their appearance drove people away. Ulcerated skin, truncated limbs, lumpy faces. People avoided lepers. But Jesus pursued them. When he heard their cry, he told them, "Go, show yourselves to the priests" (v. 14).

The lepers understood the significance of the instructions. Only the priest could reverse the stigma. To their credit the lepers obeyed.

To the credit of Jesus they were healed. As they walked, they dropped their crutches and discarded their hoods. Their spines began to straighten, skin began to clear, and smiles began to return. The mass of misery became a leaping, jumping, celebrating chorus of health.

Jesus watched them dance their way over the horizon. And he waited for their return. And he waited. And he waited. The disciples stretched out on the ground. Others went to look for food. Jesus just stood there. He wanted to hear the reunion stories. *What did your wife say? How did the kids respond? How does it feel to be healed?* Jesus waited for the ten men to return and say thanks. But only one of them came back.

> One of them, when he saw that he was healed, came back to Jesus, shouting, "Praise God, I'm healed!" He fell face down on the ground at Jesus' feet, thanking him for what he had done. This man was a Samaritan.
>
> Jesus asked, "Didn't I heal ten men? Where are the other nine? Does only this foreigner return to give glory to God?" (vv. 15–18 NLT)

Even Jesus was astonished. You'd think that neither fire nor hail could have kept them from falling at Jesus' feet. Where were the other nine? It's easy to speculate.

Some were too busy to be thankful. They planned to express thanks. But first they needed to find family members, doctors, dogs, parakeets, and neighbors. Just too busy.

Some were too cautious to be thankful. They guarded against joy, kept their hopes down. Waited for the other shoe to drop. Waited to read the fine print. Waited to see what Jesus wanted in return. What's too good to be true usually is. They were cautious.

Others were too self-centered to be thankful. The sick life was simpler. Now they had to get a job, play a role in society.

Others were too arrogant. They never were *that* sick. Given enough time, they would have recovered. Besides, to be grateful is to admit to being needy. Who wants to show weakness when you have an image to protect?

Too busy, too cautious, too self-centered, too arrogant . . . too close to home? If this story is any indication, nine out of ten people suffer from ingratitude. Epidemic proportions. Why? Why the appreciation depreciation?

I may have discovered the answer on a recent trip. I was flying home from the Midwest when a snowstorm delayed my arrival in Dallas. I raced to the gate in hopes of catching the final flight of the night for San Antonio. The airport was in a state of contained turmoil, everyone dashing to a gate. The airlines had already loaded extra passengers on my plane. With all the charm I could muster, I asked the attendant, "Are any seats left?"

She looked at her computer screen. "No," she replied, "I'm afraid . . ."

I just knew how she was going to finish the sentence: "I'm afraid you'll have to spend the night here." "I'm afraid you'll need to find a hotel." "I'm afraid you'll have to catch the 6:00 a.m. flight to San Antonio."

But she said none of these. Instead, she looked up and smiled. "I'm afraid there are no more seats in coach. We are going to have to bump you up to first class. Do you mind if we do that?"

"Do you mind if I kiss you?" So I boarded the plane and nestled down in the wide seat with the extra legroom.

Color me thankful.

Not every passenger was as appreciative as I was. A fellow across the aisle from me was angry because he had only one pillow. With the attendants scrambling to lock doors and prepare for the delayed departure, he was complaining about insufficient service. "I paid extra to fly first class. I am accustomed to better attention. I want another pillow!"

On the other side of the aisle, yours truly smiled like a guy who had won the lottery without buying a ticket. One passenger grumbled; the other was grateful. The difference? The crank paid his way into first class. My seat was a gift.

On which side of the aisle do you find yourself?

If you feel the world owes you something, brace yourself for a life of sour hours. You'll never get reimbursed. The sky will never be blue enough; the steak won't be cooked enough; the universe won't be good enough to deserve a human being like you. You'll snap and snarl your way to an early grave. "A proud man is seldom a grateful man, for he never thinks that he gets as much as he deserves."[1]

The grateful heart, on the other hand, sees each day as a gift. Thankful people focus less on the pillows they lack and more on the privileges they have. I attended a banquet recently in which a wounded soldier was presented with the gift of a free house. He nearly fell over with gratitude. He bounded onto the stage with his one good leg and threw both arms around the presenter. "Thank you! Thank you! Thank you!" He hugged the guitar player in the band and the big woman on the front row. He thanked the waiter, the other soldiers, and then the presenter again. Before the night was over, he thanked me! And I didn't do anything.

Shouldn't we be equally grateful? Jesus is building a house for us (John 14:2). Our deed of ownership is every bit as certain as that of the soldier. What's more, Jesus cured our leprosy. Sin cankered our souls and benumbed our senses. Yet the Man on the path told us we were healed, and, lo and behold, we were!

The grateful heart is like a magnet sweeping over the day, collecting reasons for gratitude. A zillion diamonds sparkle against the velvet of your sky every night. *Thank you, God.* A miracle of muscles enables your eyes to read these words and your brain to process them. *Thank you, God.* Your lungs inhale and exhale eleven thousand liters of air every day. Your heart will beat about three billion times in your lifetime. Your brain is a veritable electric generator of power. *Thank you, God.*

For the jam on our toast and the milk on our cereal. For the blanket that calms us and the joke that delights us and the warm sun that reminds us of God's love. For the thousands of planes that did not crash today. For the men who didn't cheat on their wives, and the wives who didn't turn from their men, and the kids who, in spite of unspeakable pressure to dishonor their parents, decided not to do so. *Thank you, Lord.*

Gratitude gets us through the hard stuff. To reflect on your blessings is to rehearse God's accomplishments. To rehearse God's accomplishments is to discover his heart. To discover his heart is to discover not just good gifts but the Good Giver. Gratitude always leaves us looking at God and away from dread. It does to anxiety what the morning sun does to valley mist. It burns it up.

Join the ranks of the 10 percent who give God a standing ovation. "Give thanks for everything to God the Father in the name of our Lord Jesus Christ" (Eph. 5:20 NLT).

You don't have to name a child after God, but then again, you could. Or you could draft a letter listing his blessings or write a song in his honor. You could sponsor an orphan, buy an appliance for a needy family, or adopt a child just because God adopted you. The surest path out of a slump is marked by the road sign "Thank you."

But what of the disastrous days? The nights we can't sleep and the hours we can't rest? Grateful then? Jesus was. "On the night when he was betrayed, the Lord Jesus took a loaf of bread, and when he had given thanks, he broke it" (1 Cor. 11:23–24 NLT).

Not often do you see the words *betrayed* and *thanks* in the same sentence, much less in the same heart. Jesus and the disciples were in the Upper Room. Sly Judas sat in the corner. Impetuous Peter sat at the table. One would soon betray Jesus; the other would soon curse him. Jesus knew this, yet on the night he was betrayed, he gave thanks. In the midst of the darkest night of the human soul, Jesus found a way to give thanks. Anyone can thank God for the light. Jesus teaches us to thank God for the night.

He taught eight-year-old Daniel to do so. My friend Rob cried freely as he told the story about his young son's challenging life. Daniel was born with a double cleft palate, dramatically disfiguring his face. He had surgery, but the evidence remains, so people constantly notice the difference and occasionally make remarks.

Daniel, however, is unfazed. He just tells people that God made him this way so what's the big deal? He was named student of the week at school and was asked to bring something to show his class-mates for show-and-tell. Daniel told his mom he wanted to take the pictures that showed his face prior to the surgery. His mom was concerned. "Won't that make you feel a little funny?" she asked.

But Daniel insisted. "Oh no, I want everybody to see what God did for me!"[2]

Try Daniel's defiant joy and see what happens. God has handed you a cup of blessings. Sweeten it with a heaping spoonful of gratitude.

"Let me introduce you to my sons," Joseph would tell people. "Come here, God Made Me Forget and God Made Me Fruitful. Where did I get those names? Well, have a seat, and let me tell you what God did for me."

CHAPTER 10

now, about those family scandals and scoundrels

F amily wounds are slow to heal.

I hope your childhood was a happy time when your parents kept everyone fed, safe, and chuckling. I hope your dad came home every day, your mom tucked you in bed every night, and your siblings were your best friends. I hope you find this chapter on family pain irrelevant.

But if not, you need to know you aren't alone. The most famous family tree in the Bible suffered from a serious case of blight. Adam accused Eve. Cain killed his little brother. Abraham lied about Sarah. Rebekah favored Jacob. Jacob cheated Esau and then raised a gang of hoodlums. The book of Genesis is a relative disaster.

Joseph didn't deserve to be abandoned by his brothers. True, he wasn't the easiest guy to live with. He boasted about his dreams and tattled on his siblings.[1] He deserved some of the blame for the family friction. But he certainly didn't deserve to be dumped into a pit and sold to merchants for pocket change.

The perpetrators were his ten older brothers. The eleven sons shared the same dad, dinner table, and playground. His brothers were supposed to look out for him. Joseph's next of kin were out of line. And his father? Jacob was out of touch.

With all due respect, the patriarch could have used a course on marriage and family life. Mistake number one: he married a woman he didn't love so he could marry one he did. Mistake number two:

the two wives were sisters. (Might as well toss a lit match into a fireworks stand.) The first sister bore him sons. The second sister bore him none. So to expand his clan, he slept with an assortment of handmaidens and concubines until he had a covey of kids. Rachel, his favorite wife, finally gave birth to Joseph, who became his favorite son. She later died giving birth to a second son, Benjamin, leaving Jacob with a contentious household and a broken heart.

Jacob coped by checking out. When Joseph bragged to his brothers about their bowing to him, Jacob stayed silent. When Jacob got wind that his sons had taken the sheep to graze near Shechem, the spot of prior conflict, did he spring into action to correct them? No, he sent Joseph to get a report. He sent a son to do a father's job.

Obstinate sons. Oblivious dad. The brothers needed a father. The father needed a wake-up call. And Joseph needed a protector. But he wasn't protected; he was neglected. And he landed in a distant, dark place.

Initially, Joseph chose not to face his past. By the time he saw his brothers again, Joseph had been prime minister for nearly a decade. He wore a chain of gold eagles on his neck. He bore the king's seal on his hand. The blood-bedabbled coat of colors had been replaced with the royal robe of the king. The kid from Canaan had come a long way.

Joseph could travel anywhere he wanted, yet he chose not to return to Canaan. Assemble an army and settle the score with his brothers? He had the resources. Send for his father? Or at least send a message? He'd had perhaps eight years to set the record straight. He knew where to find his family, but he chose not to contact them. He kept family secrets a secret. Untouched and untreated. Joseph was content to leave his past in the past.

But God was not. Restoration matters to God. The healing of the heart involves the healing of the past. So God shook things up.

"All countries came to Joseph in Egypt to buy grain, because the famine was severe in all lands" (Gen. 41:57). And in the long line of folks appealing for an Egyptian handout, look what the cat dragged in. "So Joseph's ten brothers went down to buy grain in Egypt" (42:3).

Joseph heard them before he saw them. He was fielding a question from a servant when he detected the Hebrew chatter. Not just the language of his heart but the dialect of his home. The prince motioned for the servant to stop speaking. He turned and looked. There they stood.

The brothers were balder, grayer, rough skinned. They were pale and gaunt with hunger. Sweaty robes clung to their shins, and road dust chalked their cheeks. These Hebrews stuck out in sophisticated Egypt like hillbillies at Times Square. When their time came to ask Joseph for grain, they didn't recognize him. His beard was shaved, his robe was royal, and the language he spoke was Egyptian. Black makeup extended from the sides of his eyes. He wore a black wig that sat on his head like a helmet. It never occurred to them that they were standing before their baby brother.

Thinking the prince couldn't understand Hebrew, the brothers spoke to him with their eyes and gestures. They pointed at the stalks of grain and then at their mouths. They motioned to the brother who carried the money, and he stumbled forward and spilled the coins on the table.

When Joseph saw the silver, his lips curled, and his stomach turned. He had named his son God Made Me Forget, but the money made him remember. The last time he saw coins in the hands of Jacob's older boys, they were laughing, and he was whimpering. That day at the pit he searched these faces for a friend, but he found none. And now they dared bring silver to him?

Joseph called for a Hebrew-speaking servant to translate. Then Joseph scowled at his brothers. "He acted as a stranger to them and spoke roughly to them" (v. 7).

I'm imagining the tone of a night watchman aroused from his midnight nap. "Who are ya? Where do ya come from?" The brothers fell face-first in the dirt, which brought to Joseph's mind a childhood dream.

"Uh, well, we're from up the road in Canaan. Maybe you've heard of it?"

Joseph glared at them. "Nah, I don't believe you. Guards, put these spies under arrest. They are here to infiltrate our country."

The ten brothers spoke at once. "You've got it all wrong, Your High, Holy, and Esteemed Honor. We're salt of the earth. We belong to the same family. That's Simeon over there. That's Judah . . . Well, there are twelve of us in all. At least there used to be. 'The youngest is now with our father, and one is no longer living'" (v. 13 HCSB).

Joseph gulped at the words. This was the first report on his family he had heard in twenty years. Jacob was alive. Benjamin was alive. And they thought he was dead.

"Tell you what," he snapped. "I'll let one of you go back and get your brother and bring him here. The rest of you I'll throw in jail."

With that, Joseph had their hands bound. A nod of his head, and they were marched off to jail. Perhaps the same jail where he had spent at least two years of his life.

What a curious series of events. The gruff voice, harsh treatment. The jail sentence. The abrupt dismissal. We've seen this sequence before with Joseph and his brothers, only the roles were reversed. On the first occasion they conspired against him. This time he conspired against them. They spoke angrily. He turned the tables. They threw him in the hole and ignored his cries for help. Now it was his turn to give them the cold shoulder.

What was going on?

I think he was trying to get his bearings. This was the toughest challenge of his life. The famine, by comparison, was easy. Mrs.

Potiphar he could resist. Pharaoh's assignments he could manage. But this mixture of hurt and hate that surged when he saw his flesh and blood? Joseph didn't know what to do.

Maybe you don't either.

Your family failed you. Your early years were hard ones. The people who should have cared for you didn't. But, like Joseph, you made the best of it. You've made a life for yourself. Even started your own family. You are happy to leave Canaan in the rearview mirror. But God isn't.

He gives us more than we request by going deeper than we ask. He wants not only your whole heart; he wants your heart whole. Why? Hurt people hurt people. Think about it. Why do you fly off the handle? Why do you avoid conflict? Why do you seek to please everyone? Might your tendencies have something to do with an unhealed hurt in your heart? God wants to help you for your sake.

And for the sake of your posterity. Suppose Joseph had refused his brothers? Summarily dismissed them? Washed his hands of the whole mess? God's plan for the nation of Israel depended upon the compassion of Joseph. A lot was at stake here.

There is a lot at stake with you too. Some years ago a dear friend of mine was called to the funeral home to identify the body of his father, who had been shot in the middle of the night by his ex-wife. The shotgun blast was just one in a long line of angry outbursts and violent family moments. My friend remembers standing near the body and resolving, *It stops with me.* (And it has.)

Make the same resolve. Yes, your family history has some sad chapters. But your history doesn't have to be your future. The generational garbage can stop here and now. You don't have to give your kids what your ancestors gave you.

Talk to God about the scandals and scoundrels. Invite him to relive the betrayal with you. Bring it out in the open. Joseph restaged the hurt for a reason. Revealing leads to healing. Don't just pray, *Lord, help me forgive my father.* Unearth the details: *God, Daddy never wanted to be a part of my life. He didn't even come to my birthday parties. I hated him for that.*

Or: *Every day I came home from school to find Mom drunk, lying on the couch. I had to make dinner, take care of baby brother, do homework on my own. It's not right, God!*

Difficult for certain. But let God do his work. The process may take a long time. It may take a lifetime. Family pain is the deepest pain because it was inflicted so early and because it involves people who should have been trustworthy. You were too young to process the mistreatment. You didn't know how to defend yourself. Besides, the perpetrators of your pain were so large. Your dad, mom, uncle, big brother—they towered over you, usually in size, always in rank.

When they judged you falsely, you believed them. All this time you've been operating on faulty data. "You're stupid . . . slow . . . dumb like your daddy . . . fat like your mama . . ." Decades later these voices of defeat still echo in your subconscious.

But they don't have to! "Let God transform you into a new person by changing the way you think" (Rom. 12:2 NLT). Let him replace childish thinking with mature truth (1 Cor. 13:11). You are not who they said you were. You are God's child. His creation. Destined for heaven. You are a part of his family. Let him set you on the path to reconciliation.

Joseph did. The process would prove to be long and difficult. It occupies four chapters of the Bible and at least a year on the calendar, but Joseph took the first step. A cautious, hesitant one but a step nonetheless. After three days Joseph released his brothers from jail. He played the tough guy again. "Go on; scoot back to—what was it, Kansas? Colorado? No, Canaan. Go on back. But I want to see this kid brother you talk about. I'll keep one of you as a guarantee."

They agreed and then, right in front of Joseph, rehashed the day they dry-gulched him: "Then they said to one another, 'We are truly guilty concerning our brother, for we saw the anguish of his soul when he pleaded with us, and we would not hear; therefore this distress has come upon us'" (Gen. 42:21).

Again, they did not know that the prince understood Hebrew. But he did. And when he heard the words, Joseph turned away so they couldn't see his eyes fill with tears. He didn't speak for a few moments, lest the lump in his throat turn into sobs unbecoming of a tough official. He stepped into the shadows and wept. He did this seven more times.[2] He didn't cry when he was promoted by Potiphar or crowned by Pharaoh, but he blubbered like a baby when he learned that his brothers hadn't forgotten him after all. When he sent them back to Canaan, he loaded their saddlebags with grain. A moment of grace.

With that small act, healing started. If God healed that family, who's to say he won't heal yours?

CHAPTER 11

revenge feels good, but then . . .

In 1882, a New York City businessman named Joseph Richardson owned a narrow strip of land on Lexington Avenue. It was 5 feet wide and 104 feet long. Another businessman, Hyman Sarner, owned a normal-sized lot adjacent to Richardson's skinny one. He wanted to build apartments that fronted the avenue. He offered Richardson $1,000 for the slender plot. Richardson was deeply offended by the amount and demanded $5,000. Sarner refused, and Richardson called Sarner a tightwad and slammed the door on him.

Sarner assumed the land would remain vacant and instructed the architect to design the apartment building with windows overlooking the avenue. When Richardson saw the finished building, he resolved to block the view. No one was going to enjoy a free view over his lot.

So seventy-year-old Richardson built a house. Five feet wide and 104 feet long and four stories high with two suites on each floor. Upon completion he and his wife moved into one of the suites.

Only one person at a time could ascend the stairs or pass through the hallway. The largest dining table in any suite was eighteen inches wide. The stoves were the very smallest made. A newspaper reporter of some girth once got stuck in the stairwell, and after two tenants were unsuccessful in pushing him free, he exited only by stripping down to his undergarments.

The building was dubbed the "Spite House." Richardson spent

the last fourteen years of his life in the narrow residence that seemed to fit his narrow state of mind.[1]

The Spite House was torn down in 1915, which is odd. I distinctly remember spending a few nights there last year. And a few weeks there some years back. If memory serves, didn't I see you squeezing through the hallway?

Revenge builds a lonely house. Space enough for one person. The lives of its tenants are reduced to one goal: make someone miserable. They do. Themselves.

No wonder God insists that we "keep a sharp eye out for weeds of bitter discontent. A thistle or two gone to seed can ruin a whole garden in no time" (Heb. 12:15 MSG).

His healing includes a move out of the house of spite, a shift away from the cramped world of grudge and toward spacious ways of grace, away from hardness and toward forgiveness. He moves us forward by healing our past.

Can he really? This mess? This history of sexual abuse? This raw anger at the father who left my mother? This seething disgust I feel every time I think of the one who treated me like yesterday's trash? Can God heal this ancient hurt in my heart?

Joseph asked these questions. You never outlive the memory of ten brothers giving you the heave-ho. They walked away and never came back. So he gave them a taste of their own medicine. When he saw them in the breadline, he snapped at them. He accused them of treachery and threw them in jail. "Take that, you rascals!"

Isn't it good to know that Joseph was human? The guy was so good it hurt. He endured slavery, succeeded in a foreign land, mastered a new language, and resisted sexual seductions. He was the model prisoner and the perfect counselor to the king. Scratch him, and he bled holy blood. We expect him to see his brothers and declare, "Father, forgive them, for they knew not what they did" (see Luke 23:34). But he didn't. He didn't because forgiving jerks is the hardest trick in the bag. We will feed the poor and counsel the king. Why, we'll memorize the book of Leviticus if God says to do so.

But . . .

"Don't let the sun go down while you are still angry" (Eph. 4:26 NLT)?

"Let all bitterness, wrath, anger, clamor, and evil speaking be put away from you, with all malice" (Eph. 4:31)?

"As Christ forgave you, so you also must do" (Col. 3:13)?

Really, God?

I have a friend who was six years old when her mother ran off with a salesman, leaving her to be raised by a good-hearted dad who knew nothing about dolls, dresses, or dates. The father and daughter stumbled through life and made the best of it. Recently the mom reappeared, like a brother out of Canaan, requested a coffee date with my friend, and said, "I'm sorry for abandoning you." The mom wants to reenter her daughter's world.

My friend's first thought was, *That's it? I'm supposed to forgive you?* Seems too easy. Doesn't the mom need to experience what she gave? A few years wondering if she will see her daughter again. Some pain-filled nights. A bit of justice. How do we reconcile the pain of the daughter with God's command to forgive? Isn't some vengeance in order?

Of course it is. In fact, God cares about justice more than we do. Paul admonished, "Never pay back evil for evil . . . never avenge yourselves. Leave that to God, for he has said that he will repay those who deserve it" (Rom. 12:17, 19 TLB).

We fear the evildoer will slip into the night, unknown and unpunished. Escape to Fiji and sip mai tais on the beach. Not to worry. Scripture says, "[God] *will* repay," not he "*might* repay." God will execute justice on behalf of truth and fairness. Case in point? Prepare yourself for the most surprising turnaround of the Joseph story.

After three days Joseph released all but one brother from jail. They returned to Canaan to report to Jacob, their father, a weak shadow of an old man. The brothers told him how Simeon was kept in Egypt as assurance they would return with Benjamin, the youngest brother. Jacob had nothing to say except, "You have bereaved me: Joseph is no more, Simeon is no more, and you want to take Benjamin. All these things are against me" (Gen. 42:36).

Such a louse. Jacob played favorites, refused to discipline, had multiple wives, and upon hearing of the imprisonment of his son, had a pity party. What a prima donna. No wonder the family was screwed up.

But as we read further, a light breaks through the clouds. Judah, who once wanted to get rid of Joseph, stepped forward. "Send [Benjamin] with me, and we will arise and go, that we may live and not die, both we and you and also our little ones. I myself will be surety for him; from my hand you shall require him. If I do not bring him back to you and set him before you, then let me bear the blame forever" (43:8–9).

Is this the same Judah? The same man who said, "Let us sell him to the Ishmaelites" (37:27)? The same brother who helped negotiate the slave trade?

Well, yes . . . and no.

Judah, as it turns out, has had his own descent into the pit. After Joseph's abduction Judah went on to have three sons. He arranged for the eldest to marry a girl named Tamar. But the son died. Following the proper protocol of his day, Judah arranged for his second son to marry Tamar. The son didn't manage the situation well and died. Judah assumed Tamar was jinxed. Afraid that his third son would meet the same fate, Judah put the matter on hold, leaving Tamar with no husband.

Later Judah's wife died. Tamar heard that Judah was coming to town. Apparently she hadn't been able to get Judah to reply to her e-mails, so she got creative. She disguised herself as a prostitute and made him an offer. Judah took the bait. He exchanged his necklace and walking stick for sex, unaware that he was sleeping with his daughter-in-law. (Oh, how lust blinds a man!) She conceived. Three months later she reappeared in Judah's life as Tamar, *pregnant* Tamar. Judah went high and mighty on her and demanded she be burned. That's when she produced Judah's necklace and walking stick, and Judah realized the child was his. He was caught in his own sin, disgraced in front of his own family.

Things had come full circle. Judah, who had deceived Jacob, was deceived. Judah, who had trapped Joseph, was trapped. Judah, who had helped humiliate Joseph, was humiliated. God gave Judah his comeuppance, and Judah came to his senses. "She has been more righteous than I," he confessed (38:26).

For years I wondered why Judah's exploits were included in the Joseph narrative. They interrupt everything. We just get started in chapter 37 with the dreams and drama of Joseph when the narrator dedicates chapter 38 to the story of Judah, the hustler, and Tamar, the faux escort. Two dead husbands. One clever widow. An odd, poorly placed story. But now I see how it fits.

For anything good to happen to Jacob's family, someone in the clan had to grow up. If not the father, one of the brothers had to mature to the point where he took responsibility for his actions. God activated the change in Judah. He gave the guy a taste of his own medicine, and the medicine worked! Judah championed the family cause. He spoke sense into his father's head. He was willing to take responsibility for Benjamin's safety and bear the blame if he failed. Judah got his wake-up call, and Joseph didn't have to lift a finger or swing a fist.

Vengeance *is* God's. He *will* repay—whether ultimately on the Day of Judgment or intermediately in this life. The point of the story? God handles all Judahs. He can discipline your abusive boss, soften your angry parent. He can bring your ex to his knees or her senses. Forgiveness doesn't diminish justice; it just entrusts it to God. He guarantees the right retribution. We give too much or too little. But the God of justice has the precise prescription.

Unlike us, God never gives up on a person. Never. Long after we have moved on, God is still there, probing the conscience, stirring conviction, always orchestrating redemption. Fix your enemies? That's God's job.

Forgive your enemies? Ah, that's where you and I come in. We forgive. "Do not let the sun go down on your anger, and do not give the devil an opportunity" (Eph. 4:26–27 NASB). The word translated *opportunity* is the Greek word *topos*,[2] the same term from which we get the English noun *topography*. It means territory or ground. Interesting. Anger gives ground to the devil. Bitterness invites him to occupy a space in your heart, to rent a room. Believe me, he will move in and stink up the place. Gossip, slander, temper—anytime you see these, Satan has claimed a bunk.

Evict him. Don't even give him the time of day. In the name of Jesus tell him to pack his bags and hit the road. Begin the process of forgiveness. Keep no list of wrongs. Pray for your antagonists rather than plot against them. Hate the wrong without hating wrongdoers. Turn your attention away from what they did *to* you to what Jesus did *for* you. Outrageous as it may seem, Jesus died for them too. If he thinks they are worth forgiving, they are. Does that make forgiveness easy? No. Quick? Seldom. Painless? It wasn't for Joseph.

The brothers returned to Egypt from Canaan, Benjamin in tow. Joseph invited them to a dinner. He asked about Jacob, spotted Benjamin, and all but came undone. "God be gracious to you, my son," he blurted before he hurried out of the room to weep (Gen. 43:29).

He returned to eat and drink and make merry with the brothers. Joseph sat them according to birth order. He singled out Benjamin for special treatment. Every time the brothers got one helping, Benjamin got five. They noticed this. But said nothing.

Joseph loaded their sacks with food and hid his personal cup in the sack of Benjamin. The brothers were barely down the road when Joseph's steward stopped their caravan, searched their sacks, and found the cup. The brothers tore their clothes (the ancient equivalent of pulling out one's hair) and soon found themselves back in front of Joseph, fearing for their lives.

Joseph couldn't make up his mind! He welcomed them, wept over them, ate with them, and then played a trick on them. He was at war with himself. These brothers had peeled the scab off his oldest and deepest wound. And he would be hanged before he'd let them do it again. On the other hand, these were his brothers, and he would be hanged before he lost them again.

Forgiveness vacillates like this. It has fits and starts, good days and bad. Anger intermingled with love. Irregular mercy. We make progress only to make a wrong turn. Step forward and fall back. But this is okay. When it comes to forgiveness, all of us are beginners. No one owns a secret formula. As long as you are trying to forgive, you are forgiving. It's when you no longer try that bitterness sets in.

Stay the course. You'll spend less time in the spite house and more in the grace house. And as one who has walked the hallways of both, I can guarantee that you are going to love the space of grace.

the prince is your brother

You've never seen a scene like this. The basketball player stands at the free throw line. His team is down by one point. Only a few seconds remain on the game clock. Players on both teams crouch, ready to grab the rebound. The shooter positions the ball in his hand. The crowd is quiet. The cheerleaders gulp. Again, you've never seen a scene like this. How can I be so sure? Because the player shooting the ball has never seen a scene like this.

He's blind.

Everyone else on his team is sighted. Everyone on the other team is sighted. But Matt Steven, a high school senior in Upper Darby, Pennsylvania, can't see a thing. His brother stands under the rim, rapping a cane on the basket. Matt listens, dribbles, and lifts the ball to shoot. We wonder, why does a basketball coach place a blind kid on the foul line?

The short answer? Because he is Matt's big brother.

The long answer began years earlier when Matt was born with two permanently detached retinas. He lost his left eye in the fifth grade and his right eye in the sixth. But even though Matt can't see, his big brother has enough vision for them both. Joe spent a childhood helping Matt do the impossible: ride a bike, ice-skate, and play soccer. So when Joe began coaching the basketball team, he brought his baby brother with him as the equipment manager. Matt never practices or plays with the team. But with Joe's help he shoots free throws after every practice. Long after the team leaves, the brothers linger—the younger one at the charity line, the older one beneath the basket, tapping a stick against the rim.

And so it is that Matt, for this tournament game, is the designated free throw shooter. Joe convinced the refs and the opponents to let Matt play. Everyone thought it was a great idea. But no one imagined the game would come down to this shot.

So far Matt is 0 for 6. The gym falls silent. Joe hits the iron rim of the basket with the cane. Up in the stands Matt's mom tries to steady the video camera. Matt dribbles. Pauses and shoots. Swish! The game is tied! The screams of the fans lift the roof of the gymnasium. Finally the crowd settles down so Matt can hear the click, and the scene-never-seen repeats itself. Swish number two! The opposing team grabs the ball and throws a Hail Mary at the other basket and misses. The game is over, and Matt is the hero. Everyone whoops and hollers while Matt—the hero—tries to find his way to the bench. Guess who comes to help him. You got it. Joe.[1]

Big brothers can make all the difference. Got bullies on your block? Big brother can protect you. Forgot your lunch money? Big brother has some extra. Can't keep your balance on your bike? He'll steady you. Call your big brother.

Big brother. Bigger than you. Stronger. Wiser.

Big *brother.* Since he is family, you are his priority. He has one job: to get you through things. Through the neighborhood, without getting lost; through the math quiz, without failing; through the shopping mall, without stopping. Big brothers walk us through the rough patches of life.

Need one? You aren't trying to make a basket, but you are trying to make a living or make a friend or make sense out of the bad breaks you've been getting. Could you use the protection of a strong sibling?

The sons of Jacob certainly needed it. As they stood before Joseph, they were the picture of pity. Accused of stealing the silver cup. Tongue-tied goat herders before a superpower sovereign. Nothing to offer but prayers, nothing to request but help. Judah told the prince their story. How their father was frail and old. How one son had perished and how also losing Benjamin would surely kill their father. Judah even offered to stay in Benjamin's place if that was what it would take to save his family. They were face-first on the floor, hoping for mercy, but they received much more.

Joseph told the officials to clear out, his translators to leave the room. "Then Joseph could not restrain himself" (Gen. 45:1). He buried his face in his hands and began to heave with emotion. He didn't weep gently or whimper softly. He wailed. The cries echoed in the palace hallways, cathartic moans of a man in a moment of deep healing. Twenty-two years of tears and trickery had come to an end. Anger and love had dueled it out. Love had won.

He broke the news: "I am Joseph; does my father still live?" (v. 3). Eleven throats gulped, and twenty-two eyes widened to the size of saucers. The brothers, still in a deep genuflect, dared not move. They ventured glances at each other and mouthed the name: *Joseph?* Their last memory of their younger brother was of a pale-faced, frightened lad being carted off to Egypt. They had counted their coins and washed their hands of the boy. He was a teenager then. He was a prince now? They lifted their heads ever so slightly.

Joseph lowered his hands. His makeup was tear smeared, and his chin still quivered. His voice shook as he spoke. "Please come near to me." They rose to their feet. Slowly. Cautiously. "I am Joseph your brother, whom you sold into Egypt" (v. 4).

Joseph told them not to fear. "God sent me here. God did this. God is protecting you" (see v. 7). In today's language, "There's more to our story than meets the eye."

The brothers were still not sure who this man was. This man who wept for them, called for them . . . and then cared for them.

Fetch your family, he instructed, and come to Egypt. He promised to provide for them and sealed the promise with even more tears. He stood from his chair and threw his arms around his baby brother. "He fell on his brother Benjamin's neck and wept . . . he kissed all his brothers and wept over them, and after that his brothers talked with him" (vv. 14–15).

One by one he received them. Judah, the one who came up with the slave trafficking idea. Reuben, the firstborn who didn't always behave like a big brother. Simeon and Levi, who wrought such violence at Shechem that their father deemed them "instruments of cruelty" (49:5).[2] Those who had tied his hands and mocked his cries. He kissed them all.

Hostility and anger melted onto the marble floor. Joseph didn't talk at them or over them. They just talked. "How's Dad? Reuben, you're looking chubby. Simeon, how's your health? Levi, did you ever marry that girl from across the field? Have any kids? Any grandkids?"

When Pharaoh heard about Joseph's siblings, Pharaoh told him, "Any family of yours is a family of mine." And the next thing you know, Joseph was outfitting his brothers in new clothes and carts. They were honorary citizens of Egypt. Outcasts one moment. People of privilege the next.

At about this point the brothers began to realize they were out of danger. The famine still raged. The fields still begged. Circumstances were still hostile. But they were finally safe. They would make it through this. Because they were good men? No, because they were family. The prince was their brother.

Oh, for such a gift. We know the feel of a famine. Like the brothers of Joseph, we've found ourselves in dry seasons. Resources gone.

Supplies depleted. Energy expired. We've stood where the brothers stood.

We've done what the brothers did. We've hurt the people we love. Sold them into slavery? Maybe not. But lost our temper? Misplaced our priorities? You bet. Like the shepherds of Beersheba, we've sought help from the Prince, our Prince. We've offered our prayers and pleaded our cases. We've wondered if he would have a place for the likes of us. What the brothers found in Joseph's court we find in Jesus Christ. The Prince is our brother.

Is this a new thought for you? You've heard Jesus described as King, Savior, and Lord, but Brother? This is biblical language. On one occasion Jesus was speaking to his followers when his family tried to get his attention. His mother and brothers stood outside and sent word that they wanted to speak to him. Jesus took advantage of the moment to make a tender gesture and statement. "He stretched out His hand toward His disciples and said, 'Here are My mother and My brothers! For whoever does the will of My Father in heaven is My brother and sister and mother'" (Matt. 12:49–50).

Had you and I been present that day, we would have looked at the "family" of Jesus and seen little to impress us. None of his followers was of noble birth. No deep pockets or blue blood. Peter had his swagger. John had his temper. Matthew had his checkered past and colorful friends. Like Jacob's sons in the Egyptian court, they seemed outclassed and out of place. Yet Jesus was not embarrassed to call them his family. He laid claim to them in public. He lays claim to us as well. "Jesus, who makes people holy, and those who are made holy are from the same family. So he is not ashamed to call them his brothers and sisters" (Heb. 2:11 NCV).

Jesus redefined his family to include all who come near him.

The account of Joseph is simply an appetizer for the Bible's main course, the story of Jesus. So many similarities exist between the two men. Joseph was the favorite son of Jacob. Jesus was the beloved Son of God (Matt. 3:17). Joseph wore the coat of many colors. Jesus did the deeds of many wonders. Joseph fed the nations. Jesus fed the multitudes. Joseph prepared his people for the coming famine. Jesus came to prepare his people for eternity. Under Joseph's administration grain increased. In Jesus' hands water became the finest wine, and a basket of bread became a buffet for thousands. Joseph responded to a crisis of nature. Jesus responded to one crisis after another. He told typhoons to settle down and waves to be quiet. He commanded cadavers to stand up, the crippled to dance a jig, and the mute to sing an anthem.

And people hated him for it.

Joseph was sold for twenty pieces of silver, Jesus for thirty. Joseph was falsely accused and thrown into a prison. Jesus was condemned for no cause and nailed to a cross. The brothers thought they had seen the last of Joseph. The soldiers sealed the tomb, thinking the same about Jesus. But Joseph resurfaced as a prince. So did Jesus. While his killers slept and followers wept, Jesus stood up from the slab of death. He unwrapped his burial clothes and stepped out into the Sunday morning sunrise.

God gave Jesus what Pharaoh gave Joseph: a promotion to the highest place. "God raised him from death and set him on a throne in deep heaven, in charge of running the universe, everything from galaxies to governments, no name and no power exempt from his rule. And not just for the time being, but *forever*. He is in charge of it all, has the final word on everything" (Eph. 1:20–22 MSG).

This is where the similarities cease. Joseph's reign and life eventually ended. But Jesus'? Heaven will never see an empty throne. Jesus occupies it at this very moment. He creates weather patterns, redirects calendars, and recycles calamities—all with the goal of creating moments like this one in which we, his undeserving family, can hear him say, "I am Jesus, your Brother."

He weeps at the very sight of you. Not tears of shame but tears of joy.

He calls for you. "Come to me, all of you who are weary and carry heavy burdens, and I will give you rest" (Matt. 11:28 NLT). One foot of distance is too much. He wants us to come near. All of us. We who threw him into the pit. We who sold him out for silver. We who buried the very memory of our deeds. *Come. Come. Come.*

He cares for you. Joseph spoke to his king, and Jesus speaks to ours. In him "we have an Advocate with the Father, Jesus Christ the righteous" (1 John 2:1). Joseph gave his brothers wagons and robes. Your Brother promises to "supply all your need according to His riches" (Phil. 4:19).

Let's trust him to take care of us.

God is doing in our generation what he did in ancient Egypt: redeeming a remnant of people. In his final book God reiterates his vision: "A great multitude which no one could number, of all nations, tribes, peoples, and tongues, standing before the throne and before the Lamb, clothed with white robes, with palm branches in their hands, and crying out with a loud voice, saying, 'Salvation belongs to our God who sits on the throne, and to the Lamb!'" (Rev. 7:9–10).

This dream drives the heart of God. His purpose from all eternity is to prepare a family to indwell the kingdom of God. "'I know the *plans* I have for you,' declares the LORD, '*plans* to prosper you and not to harm you, *plans* to give you hope and a future'" (Jer. 29:11 NIV).[3] Oh, the beauty of the thrice-repeated word *plans*. God is plotting for our good. In all the setbacks and slipups, he is ordaining the best for our future. Every event of our days is designed to draw us toward our God and our destiny.

To the degree that we believe and accept his vision for our lives, we will get through life. When people junk us into the pit, we will stand up. *God can use this for good.* When family members sell us out, we will climb to our feet. *God will recycle this pain.* Falsely accused? Wrongly imprisoned? Utterly abandoned? We may stumble, but we do not fall. Why? "[God] works out everything in conformity with the purpose of his will" (Eph. 1:11 NIV). *Everything* means everything. No exceptions. Everything in your life is leading to a climactic moment in which Jesus will "reconcile to himself all things, whether things on earth or things in heaven, by making peace through his blood, shed on the cross" (Col. 1:20 NIV).

At the right time, in God's timing, you will be taken home to Canaan. But till then, stay close to your Brother.

After Matt Stevens made the foul shots, he became the hero of his high school. Everyone wanted to meet him. Cheerleaders wanted to talk to him. It was reported that he was thinking about asking a girl to the prom. Wonderful things happen when a big brother helps out.

You will get through this. Not because you are strong but because your Brother is. Not because you are good but because your Brother is. Not because you are big but because your big Brother is the Prince, and he has a place prepared for you.

good-bye to good-byes

J ohn Glenn knows how to fly a fighter jet. He completed fifty-nine missions in World War II and ninety in the Korean War. He knows how to fly fast. He was the first pilot to average supersonic speed on a transcontinental flight. He knows how to fly into outer space. In 1962 he became the first American to orbit the earth.[1] John Glenn knows how to win elections. He was a United States senator from 1974 to 1999.

John Glenn can do much. Give speeches, lead committees, inspire audiences, and write books. Yet for all his accomplishments, there is one skill he never mastered. He never learned to tell his wife good-bye.

The two met when they were toddlers and grew up together in New Concord, Ohio. Though John went on to achieve national fame, he would tell you that the true hero of the family is the girl he married in 1943.

Annie suffered from such severe stuttering that 85 percent of her efforts to speak fell short. She couldn't talk on the phone, order food in a restaurant, or give verbal instructions to a taxi driver. The idea of requesting help in a department store intimidated her. She would wander the aisles, reluctant to speak. She feared the possibility of a family crisis because she didn't know if she could make the 911 call.

Hence the difficulty with *good-bye*. John couldn't bear the thought of separation. So the two developed a code. Each time he was deployed on a mission or called to travel, the couple bid each other farewell the same way. "I'm just going down to the corner store to get a pack of gum," he would say. "Don't be long," she'd reply. And off he would go to Japan, Korea, or outer space.

Over the years Annie's speech improved. Intense therapy clarified her enunciation skills and improved her confidence. Even so, *good-bye* was the one word the couple could not say to each other. In 1998, Senator Glenn became the oldest astronaut in history. He reentered space aboard the shuttle *Discovery*. Upon departure he told his wife, "I'm just going down to the corner store to get a pack of gum." This time he gave her a present: a pack of gum. She kept it in a pocket near her heart until he was safely home.[2]

Good-bye. No one wants to say it. Not the spouse of an astronaut. Not the mom of a soon-to-be preschooler. Not the father of the bride. Not the husband in the convalescent home. Not the wife in the funeral home.

Especially not her. Death is the most difficult good-bye of all. I write these words freshly reminded of the ache of saying good-bye. Our church has had five funerals in the last seven days, from the memorial for a baby to the burial of a ninety-four-year-old friend. The sorrow took its toll on me. I found myself moping about, sad. I chided myself, *Come on, Max. Get over it. Death is a natural part of living.*

Then I self-corrected. *No, it isn't.* Birth is. Breathing is. Belly laughs, big hugs, and bedtime kisses are. But death? We were not made to say good-bye. God's original plan had no farewell—no final breath, day, or heartbeat.

Death is the interloper, the intruder, the stick-figure sketch in the Louvre. It doesn't fit. Why would God give a fishing buddy and then take him? Fill a crib and then empty it? No matter how you frame it, *good-bye* doesn't feel right.

Jacob and Joseph lived beneath the shadow of *good-bye.* When the brothers lied about Joseph's death, they gave Jacob a blood-soaked tunic. A wild beast dragged the body away, they implied. Jacob collapsed in sorrow. "Then Jacob tore his clothes, put on sackcloth and mourned for his son many days" (Gen. 37:34 NIV).

Jacob wept until the tears turned to brine, until his soul shriveled. The two people he loved the most were gone. Rachel dead. Joseph dead. Jacob, it seems, died. "All his sons and daughters came to comfort him, but he refused to be comforted. 'No,' he said, 'in mourning will I go down to the grave to my son.' So his father wept for him" (v. 35 NIV).

Joseph lived with the same sorrow. Two decades passed. No word from home. Birthdays, holidays, harvest days. Jacob was never far from his thoughts.

The moment Joseph revealed his identity to his brothers, he asked, "I am Joseph; does my father still live?" (45:3).

Question number one: "How's Dad?" Priority number one: a family reunion. Joseph told his brothers to saddle up, ship out, and come back with the entire family.

> He supplied them with provisions for the journey. And he gave each of them new clothes—but to Benjamin he gave five changes of clothes and three hundred pieces of silver! He sent his father ten donkeys loaded with the good things of Egypt, and ten donkeys loaded with grain and all kinds of other food to be eaten on his journey. So he sent his brothers off, and as they left, he called after them, "Don't quarrel along the way!" And they left Egypt and returned to their father, Jacob, in the land of Canaan. (vv. 21–25 NLT)

Jacob's boys returned to Canaan in style. Gone were the shabby robes and emaciated donkeys. They drove brand-new pickup trucks packed with gifts. They wore leather jackets and alligator skin boots.

Their wives and kids spotted them on the horizon. "You're back! You're back!" Hugs and backslaps all around.

Jacob emerged from a tent. A rush of hair, long and silver, reached his shoulders. Stooped back. Face leathery, like rawhide. He squinted at the sun-kissed sight of his sons and all the plunder. He was just about to ask where they stole the stuff when one of them blurted, "'Joseph is still alive, and he is governor over all the land of Egypt.' And Jacob's heart stood still, because he did not believe them" (v. 26).

The old man grabbed his chest. He had to sit down. Leah brought him some water and glared at the sons as if to say they had better not be playing a joke on their father. But this was no trick. "When they told him all the words which Joseph had said to them, and when he saw the carts which Joseph had sent to carry him, the spirit of Jacob their father revived" (v. 27).

Sadness had sapped the last drop of joy out of Jacob. Yet when the sons told him what Joseph had said, how he had asked about Jacob, how he had called them to Egypt, Jacob's spirit revived. He looked at the prima facie evidence of carts and clothes. He looked at the confirming smiles and nods of his sons, and for the first time in more than twenty years, the old patriarch began to believe he would see his son again.

His eyes began to sparkle, and his shoulders straightened. "Then Israel said, 'It is enough. Joseph my son is still alive. I will go and see him before I die'" (v. 28). Yes, the narrator calls Jacob by his other name (Gen. 32:28). The promise of a family reunion can do this. It changes us. From sad to seeking. From lonely to longing. From hermit to pilgrim. From Jacob (the heel grabber) to Israel (prince of God).

"So Israel took his journey with all that he had, and came to Beersheba, and offered sacrifices to the God of his father Isaac" (46:1). Jacob was 130 years old by this point. Hardly a spring chicken. He had a hitch in his "getalong," an ache in his joints. But nothing was going to keep him from his son. He took his staff in hand and issued the command: "Load 'em up! We are headed to Egypt."

The text goes to wide-angle at this point, and we are given an aerial view of the entire clan in migration. By virtue of a census, the narrator mentions each family member by name. The sons, the wives, the children. No one left out. The whole gang of seventy made the trip.

And what a trip it was. Pyramids. Palaces. Irrigated farms. Silos. They had never seen such sights. Then the moment they'd been waiting for: a wide flank of royalty appeared on the horizon. Chariots, horses, and the Imperial Guard.

As the entourage drew near, Jacob leaned forward to get a better glimpse of the man in the center chariot. When he saw his face, Jacob whispered, "Joseph, my son."

Across the distance Joseph leaned forward in his chariot. He told his driver to slap the horse. When the two groups met on the flat of the plain, the prince didn't hesitate. He bounded out of his chariot and ran in the direction of his father. "The moment Joseph saw him, he threw himself on his neck and wept" (v. 29 MSG).

Gone were the formalities. Forgotten were the proprieties. Joseph buried his face in the crook of his father's shoulder. "He wept a long time" (v. 29 MSG). As tears moistened the robe of his father, both men resolved that they would never say good-bye to each other again.

Good-bye. For some of you this word is the challenge of your life. To get through this is to get through raging loneliness, strength-draining grief. You sleep alone in a double bed. You walk the hallways of a silent house. You catch yourself calling out his name or reaching for her hand. As with Jacob, the separation has exhausted your spirit. You feel quarantined, isolated. The rest of the world has moved on; you ache to do the same. But you can't; you can't say good-bye.

If you can't, take heart. God has served notice. All farewells are on the clock. They are filtering like grains of sand through an hourglass.

If heaven's throne room has a calendar, one day is circled in red and highlighted in yellow. God has decreed a family reunion.

> The Master himself will give the command. Archangel thunder! God's trumpet blast! He'll come down from heaven and the dead in Christ will rise—they'll go first. Then the rest of us who are still alive at the time will be caught up with them into the clouds to meet the Master. Oh, we'll be walking on air! And then there will be one huge family reunion with the Master. So reassure one another with these words. (1 Thess. 4:16–18 MSG)

This day will be no small day. It will be the Great Day. The archangel will inaugurate it with a trumpet blast. Thousands and thousands of angels will appear in the sky (Jude 14–15). Cemeteries and seas will give up their dead. "Christ . . . will appear a second time, not to deal with sin but to save those who are eagerly waiting for him" (Heb. 9:28 ESV).

His coming will be the only event witnessed by all humanity. "Every eye will see Him" (Rev. 1:7). Moses will be watching. Napoleon's head will turn. The eyes of Martin Luther and Christopher Columbus will widen. The wicked despot of hades. The white-robed martyr of paradise. From Adam to the baby born as the trumpet blares, everyone will witness the moment.

Not everyone will want the moment, however. "Unready people all over the world . . . will raise a huge lament as they watch the Son of Man blazing out of heaven" (Matt. 24:30 MSG). Just as the book of Genesis lists the family of Jacob, the Book of Life lists the family of God. He will call the name of every person who accepted his invitation. He will honor the request of those who refused him and dismiss them for eternity. Then he will bless the desire of those who accepted him and gather them for a family reunion.

What a reunion it will be. "He will wipe every tear from their eyes" (Rev. 21:4 NIV). His first action will be to rub a thumb across the cheek of every child as if to say, "There, there . . . no more tears." This long journey will come to an end. You will see him.

And you will see *them.* Isn't this our hope? "There will be one huge family reunion with the Master. So reassure one another with these words" (1 Thess. 4:17–18 MSG).

Steven Curtis Chapman and his wife, Mary Beth, are banking on this promise. In May 2008 their beautiful five-year-old daughter was killed in an automobile accident. Since Steven is an internationally known and beloved Christian singer, words of support and concern poured in from all over the globe. Letters, e-mails, phone calls. The Chapmans were deluged by messages of kindness. One conversation in particular gave Steven strength. Pastor Greg Laurie, who had lost a son in an auto accident, told Steven, "Remember, your future with Maria is infinitely greater than your past with her."[3]

Death seems to take so much. We bury not just a body but the wedding that never happened, the golden years we never knew. We bury dreams. But in heaven these dreams will come true. God has promised a "restoration of all things" (Acts 3:21 ASV). "All things" includes all relationships.

Colton Burpo was only four years old when he survived an emergency appendectomy. His parents were overjoyed at his survival. But they were stunned at his stories. Over the next few months Colton talked of his visit to heaven. He described exactly what his parents were doing during the surgery and told stories of people he had met in heaven—people he had never met on earth or been told about. In the book *Heaven Is for Real,* Colton's father relates the moment that the four-year-old boy told his mom, "You had a baby die in your tummy, didn't you?"

The parents had never mentioned the miscarriage to their son. He was too young to process it. Emotion filled his mother's face.

"Who told you I had a baby die in my tummy?" Sonja said, her tone serious.

"She did, Mommy. She said she died in your tummy." . . .

A bit nervously, Colton . . . faced his mom again, this time more warily. "It's okay, Mommy," he said. "She's okay. God adopted her."

Sonja slid off the couch and knelt down in front of Colton so that she could look him in the eyes. "Don't you mean Jesus adopted her?" she said.

"No, Mommy. His Dad did!" . . .

Sonja's eyes lit up, and she asked, "What was her name? What was the little girl's name?"

. . . "She doesn't have a name. You guys didn't name her."

The parents were stunned. There is no way Colton would have known this.

But he had one more memory. He shared it before he went out to play: "Yeah, she said she just can't wait for you and Daddy to get to heaven."[4]

Someone in heaven is saying the same words about you. Your grandpa? Aunt? Your child? They are looking toward the day when God's family is back together. Shouldn't we do the same? "Since we are surrounded by such a huge crowd of witnesses . . . let us run with endurance the race that God has set before us" (Heb. 12:1 NLT). High above us there is a crowd of witnesses. They are the Abrahams, Jacobs, and Josephs from all generations and nations. They have completed their own events and now witness the races of their spiritual, if not physical, descendants. *Listen carefully*, the passage compels, *and you will hear a multitude of God's children urging you on.* "Run!" they shout. "Run! You'll get through this!"

Our final home will hear no *good-byes*. We will speak of the Good Book and remember good faith, but *good-bye*? Gone forever.

Let the promise change you. From sagging to seeking, from mournful to hopeful. From dwellers in the land of good-bye to a heaven of hellos. The Prince has decreed a homecoming. Let's take our staffs and travel in his direction.

keep calm and carry on

S ee the hole in the skyline?"

I leaned forward and followed the finger of the driver. He was a rotund guy named Frank. Neck too big for his collar, hands too thick to wrap around the steering wheel. He pointed through the windshield at the forest of buildings called Lower Manhattan.

"The towers used to sit right there."

He could tell that I couldn't see the spot.

"See the hole to the left of the one with the spire? Three days ago that was the World Trade Center. I looked at it each day as I came over the bridge. It was a powerful sight. The first morning I entered the city and saw no towers, I called my wife and cried."

To reach the epicenter of activity, we drove through layers of inactivity. Empty ambulances lined the road. Loved ones mingled outside the Family Care Center, where the USNS *Comfort*, a hospital ship, sat docked. Everyone waited. But each passing second took with it a grain of hope.

Three checkpoints later we parked the car and walked the final half mile. A week earlier this road had been full of flannel suits, cell phones, and market quotes. But on this day the sidewalk was muddy, and the air was thick with smoke. I decided not to think about what I was inhaling.

I didn't expect the fires. In spite of the rain and truckloads of water, flames still danced. I didn't anticipate the adjoining damage.

Neighboring buildings were devastated. Intact windows were rare. The next-door Marriott had been gutted by the cockpit of a jet. Any other day it would have made the cover of a magazine.

But most of all I didn't expect the numbness. Not theirs, not mine. A flank of yellow-suited firemen, some twelve or so in width, marched past us. The same number walked toward us. Shift change. Those coming were grim. Those leaving were more so, faces as steely as the beams that coffined their comrades.

My response wasn't any different. No tears. No lump in the throat. Just numbness. *Several thousand people are under there*, I told myself. Yet I just stared. The tragedy spoke a language I'd never studied. I half expected—and even more, wanted—to hear someone yell, "Quiet on the set!" and see actors run out of the ruins. But the cranes carried no cameras, just concrete.

Later that night I spoke with an officer who guarded the entrance to the Family Care Center. He was posted next to the plywood wall of photos—the wailing wall, of sorts—on which relatives had tacked pictures and hopes. I asked him to describe the expressions on the faces of the people who had come to look at the pictures.

"Blank," he said. "Blank."

"They don't cry?"

"They don't cry."

"And you, have you cried?"

"Not yet. I just push it in."

Disbelief, for many, was the drug of choice.

We can relate. Calamities can leave us off balance and confused.

Consider the crisis of Joseph's generation. "Now there was no bread in all the land; for the famine was very severe, so that the land of Egypt and the land of Canaan languished because of the famine" (Gen. 47:13).

During the time Joseph was struggling to reconcile with his

brothers, he was also navigating a catastrophe. It had been two years since the last drop of rain. The sky was endlessly blue. The sun relentlessly hot. Animal carcasses littered the ground, and no hope appeared on the horizon. The land was a dust bowl. No rain meant no farming. No farming meant no food. When people appealed to Pharaoh for help, he said, "Go to Joseph; whatever he says to you, do" (41:55).

Joseph faced a calamity on a global scale.

Yet contrast the description of the problem with the outcome. Years passed, and the people told Joseph, "You have saved our lives; let us find favor in the sight of my lord, and we will be Pharaoh's servants" (47:25).

The people remained calm. A society that was ripe for bedlam actually thanked the government rather than attacked it. Makes a person wonder if Joseph ever taught a course in crisis management. If he did, he included the words he told his brothers: "God sent me before you to preserve life. For these two years the famine has been in the land, and there are still five years in which there will be neither plowing nor harvesting. And God sent me before you" (45:5–7).

Joseph began and ended his crisis assessment with references to God. God preceded the famine. God would outlive the famine. God was all over the famine. "God . . . famine . . . God."

How would you describe your crisis?

"The economy . . . the economy . . . the economy . . . the economy."

"The divorce . . . divorce . . . divorce . . . divorce."

"Cranky spouse . . . cranky spouse . . . cranky spouse . . . cranky spouse."

Do you recite your woes more naturally than you do heaven's strength? If so, no wonder life is tough. You're assuming God isn't in this crisis.

He is. Even a famine was fair game for God's purpose.

I enjoyed breakfast recently with a friend. Most of our talk revolved around the health of his fourteen-year-old son. Seven years ago a tumor was found behind the boy's spleen. The discovery led to several months of strenuous prayer and chemotherapy. The son recovered. He is now playing high school football, and the cancer clinic is a distant memory.

The discovery of the tumor was the part of the story I found fascinating. When the boy was seven years old, he was horsing around with his cousins. One of them accidentally kicked him in the stomach. Acute pain led to a hospital visit. An alert doctor requested a series of tests. And the tests led the surgeon to discover and remove the tumor. After the cancer was removed, the father asked the physician how long the tumor had been present. Although it was impossible to know with certainty, the form and size of the tumor indicated it was no more than two or three days old.

"So," I said, "God used a kick in the gut to get your boy into treatment."

Then there is the story of Isabel. She spent the first three and a half years of her life in a Nicaraguan orphanage. No mother, no father. No promise of either. With all orphans, odds of adoption diminish with time. Every passing month decreased Isabel's chance of being placed in a home.

And then a door slammed on her finger. She was following the other children into the yard to play when a screen door closed on her hand. Pain shot up her arm, and her scream echoed across the playground. Question: Why would God let this happen? Why would a benevolent, omnipotent God permit an innocent girl with more than her share of challenges to feel additional pain?

Might he be calling for the attention of Ryan Schnoke, the American would-be father who was sitting in the playroom nearby? He and his wife, Cristina, had been trying to adopt a child for months. No other adult was around to help Isabel, so Ryan walked over, picked her up, and comforted her.

Several months later when Ryan and Cristina were close to giving up, Ryan remembered Isabel and resolved to try one more time. This time the adoption succeeded. Little Isabel is growing up in a happy, healthy home.

A kick in the gut?

A finger in the door?

God doesn't manufacture pain, but he certainly puts it to use. "God . . . is the blessed controller of all things" (1 Tim. 6:15 PHILLIPS). His ways are higher than ours (Isa. 55:9). His judgments are unsearchable, and his paths are beyond tracing out (Rom. 11:33). We can't always see what God is doing, but can't we assume he is up to something good? Joseph did. He assumed God was in the crisis.

Then he faced the crisis with a plan. He collected grain during the good years and redistributed it in the bad. When the people ran out of food, he gave it to them in exchange for money, livestock, and property. After he stabilized the economy, he gave the people a lesson in money management. "Give one-fifth to Pharaoh, and use the rest for farming and eating" (Gen. 47:24, author's paraphrase).

The plan could fit on an index card. "Save for seven years. Distribute for seven years. Manage carefully." Could his response have been simpler?

Could it have been more boring?

Some flamboyance would have been nice. A little bit of the Red Sea opening, Jericho's walls tumbling, or was-dead Lazarus walking. A dramatic crisis requires a dramatic response, right? Not always.

We equate spirituality with high drama: Paul raising the dead, Peter healing the sick. Yet for every Paul and Peter, there are a dozen Josephs. Men and women blessed with skills of administration. Steady hands through whom God saves people. Joseph never raised the dead, but he kept people from dying. He never healed the sick, but he kept sickness from spreading. He made a plan and stuck with it. And because he did, the nation survived. He triumphed with a calm, methodical plan.

In the days leading up to the war with Germany, the British government commissioned a series of posters. The idea was to capture encouraging slogans on paper and distribute them about the country. Capital letters in a distinct typeface were used, and a simple two-color format was selected. The only graphic was the crown of King George VI.

The first poster was distributed in September of 1939:

YOUR COURAGE
YOUR CHEERFULNESS
YOUR RESOLUTION
WILL BRING
US VICTORY

Soon thereafter a second poster was produced:

FREEDOM IS
IN PERIL
DEFEND IT
WITH ALL
YOUR MIGHT

These two posters appeared up and down the British countryside. On railroad platforms and in pubs, stores, and restaurants. They were everywhere. A third poster was created yet never distributed. More than 2.5 million copies were printed yet never seen until nearly sixty years later when a bookstore owner in northeast England discovered one in a box of old books he had purchased at an auction. It read:

KEEP

CALM

AND

CARRY

ON

The poster bore the same crown and style of the first two posters. It was never released to the public, however, but was held in reserve for an extreme crisis, such as invasion by Germany. The bookstore owner framed it and hung it on the wall. It became so popular that the bookstore began producing identical images of the original design on coffee mugs, postcards, and posters. Everyone, it seems, appreciated the reminder from another generation to keep calm and carry on.[1]

Of all the Bible heroes, Joseph is the one most likely to have hung a copy on his office wall. He indwelt the world of ledgers, flow-charts, end-of-the-year reports, tabulations, and calculations. Day after day. Month after month. Year after year. He kept a cool head and carried on.

You can do the same. You can't control the weather. You aren't in charge of the economy. You can't undo the tsunami or unwreck the car, but you can map out a strategy. Remember, God is in this crisis. Ask him to give you an index card–sized plan, two or three steps you can take today.

Seek counsel from someone who has faced a similar challenge. Ask friends to pray. Look for resources. Reach out to a support group. Most importantly, make a plan.

Management guru Jim Collins has some good words here. He and Morten T. Hansen studied leadership in turbulent times. They looked at more than twenty thousand companies, sifting through data in search of an answer to this question: Why in uncertain times do some companies thrive while others do not? They concluded, "[Successful leaders] are not more creative. They're not more visionary. They're not more charismatic. They're not more ambitious. They're not more blessed by luck. They're not more risk-seeking. They're not more heroic. And they're not more prone to making big, bold moves." Then what sets them apart? "They all led their teams with a surprising method of self-control in an out-of-control world."[2]

In the end it's not the flashy and flamboyant who survive. It is those with steady hands and sober minds. People like Roald Amundsen. In 1911, he headed up the Norwegian team in a race to the South Pole. Robert Scott directed a team from England. The two expeditions faced identical challenges and terrain. They endured the same freezing temperatures and unforgiving environment. They had equal access to the technology and equipment of their day. Yet Amundsen and his team reached the South Pole thirty-four days ahead of Scott. What made the difference?

Planning. Amundsen was a tireless strategist. He had a clear strategy of traveling fifteen to twenty miles a day. Good weather? Fifteen to twenty miles. Bad weather? Fifteen to twenty miles. No more. No less. Always fifteen to twenty miles.

Scott, by contrast, was irregular. He pushed his team to exhaustion in good weather and stopped in bad. The two men had two different philosophies and, consequently, two different outcomes. Amundsen won the race without losing a man. Scott lost not only the race but also his life and the lives of all his team members.[3]

All for the lack of a good plan.

You'd prefer a miracle for your crisis? You'd rather see the bread multiplied or the stormy sea turned glassy calm in a finger snap? God may do this.

Then, again, he may tell you, "I'm with you. I can use this for good. Now let's make a plan." Trust him to help you.

God's sovereignty doesn't negate our responsibility. Just the opposite. It empowers it. When we trust God, we think more clearly and react more decisively. Like Nehemiah, who said, "We prayed to our God and posted a guard day and night to meet this threat" (Neh. 4:9 NIV).

We prayed . . . and posted. We trusted and acted. Trust God to do what you can't. Obey God, and do what you can.

Don't let the crisis paralyze you. Don't let the sadness overwhelm you. Don't let the fear intimidate you. To do nothing is the wrong thing. To do something is the right thing. And to believe is the highest thing. Just . . .

KEEP
CALM
AND
CARRY
ON

evil. God. good.

L ife turns every person upside down. No one escapes unscathed. Not the woman who discovers her husband is having an affair. Not the businessman whose investments are embezzled by a crooked colleague. Not the teenager who discovers that a night of romance has resulted in a surprise pregnancy. Not the pastor who feels his faith shaken by questions of suffering and fear.

We'd be foolish to think we are invulnerable.

But we'd be just as foolish to think that evil wins the day.

The Bible vibrates with the steady drumbeat of faith: God recycles evil into righteousness. Perhaps you read this book in search of a quick fix for your challenges. "How to Overcome Obstacles in Five Easy Steps." Sorry to disappoint. I don't have an easy solution or a magic wand. I have found something—Someone—far better. God himself. When God gets in the middle of life, evil becomes good.

Haven't we discovered this in the story of Joseph? Saddled with setbacks: family rejection, deportation, slavery, and imprisonment. Yet he emerged triumphant, a hero of his generation. Among his final recorded words are these comments to his brothers: "You meant evil against me; but God meant it for good" (Gen. 50:20).

This is the repeated pattern in Scripture: *Evil. God. Good.*

Evil came to Job. Tempted him, tested him. Job struggled. But God countered. He spoke truth. Declared sovereignty. Job in the end chose God. Satan's prime target became God's star witness. Good resulted.

Evil came to Moses. Convinced him to murder an Egyptian guard, liberate a people with anger. God countered. He placed Moses on a forty-year cooldown. Moses in the end chose God. He liberated like a shepherd, not a soldier. Good resulted.

Evil came to David: he committed adultery;

to Daniel: he was dragged to a foreign land;

to Nehemiah: the walls of Jerusalem were destroyed.

But God countered. And because he did,

David wrote songs of grace,

Daniel ruled in a foreign land, and

Nehemiah rebuilt Jerusalem's walls with Babylonian lumber.

Good happened.

And Jesus. How many times in his earthly life did bad become good?

The Bethlehem innkeeper told Jesus' parents to try their luck in the barn. That was bad. God entered the world in the humblest place on earth. That was good.

The wedding had no wine. Bad. The wedding guests witnessed the first miracle of Jesus. Good.

The storm scared the faith out of the apostles. Bad. The sight of water-walking Jesus turned them into worshippers. Good.

Five thousand men needed food for their families. Bad day to be a disciple. Jesus turned a basket into a bakery. Good day to be a disciple.

With Jesus, bad became good just as night becomes day—regularly, reliably, refreshingly. And redemptively.

See the cross on the hill? Can you hear the soldiers pound the nails? Jesus' enemies smirk. Satan's demons lurk. All that is evil rubs its hands in glee. "This time," Satan whispers. "This time I will win."

For a sad Friday and a silent Saturday it appeared he had. The final breath. The battered body. Mary wept. Blood seeped down the timber into the dirt. Followers lowered God's Son before the sun set. Soldiers sealed the tomb, and night fell over the earth.

Yet what Satan intended as the ultimate evil, God used for the ultimate good. God rolled the rock away. Jesus walked out on Sunday morning, a smile on his face and a bounce to his steps. And if you look closely, you can see Satan scampering from the cemetery with his forked tail between his legs.

"Will I ever win?" he grumbles.

No. He won't. The stories of Jesus, Joseph, and a thousand others assure us that what Satan intends for evil, God uses for good.

My friend Christine Caine is walking proof of this promise. She is an Australian spark plug. Five feet three inches of energy, passion, and love. To sit down with Christine is to share a meal with a modern-day Joseph. She is at war with one of the greatest calamities of our generation: sex slavery. She travels three hundred days a year. She meets with cabinets, presidents, and parliaments. She stares down pimps and defies organized crime. With God as her helper, she will see sex slavery brought to its knees.

Pretty impressive for a girl whose world was turned upside down. At the age of thirty she stumbled upon the stunning news of her adoption. The couple who raised her never intended for her to know. When Christine happened upon the truth, she tracked down her biological parents.

The official records of her birth told her this much: she was born to a Greek mother named Panagiota. The box designated "Father's Name" bore the word "Unknown." Christine recounts how she "lingered over this word, trying to understand how someone so important to me could be reduced to simply this . . . Seven letters, one word, and that single word seemed so inadequate."[1]

But there was more. Next to the box marked "Child's Name" was another seven-letter word. It sucked the air out of Christine. "Unnamed."

Father "unknown." Child "unnamed." According to the document, Christine Caine was simply this: "birth number 2508 of the year 1966."[2]

Abandoned by those who conceived and bore you. Could anything be worse? Actually, yes. To be sexually abused by members of your family. Time and time again they took advantage of her. They turned her childhood into a horror story of one encounter after another. Twelve years of unbridled and ugly evil.

Yet what they intended for evil, God used for good. Christine chose to heed not the hurts of her past but the promise of her heavenly Father. She laid hold of Isaiah 49: "The LORD has called Me from the womb; from the matrix of My mother He has made mention of My name" (v. 1). Christine made a Joseph-like decision to believe in the God who believed in her.

Years later when she heard of the plight of girls caught in the sex trade, she knew she had to respond. When she saw their faces on missing-person posters and heard of the abuse at the hands of captors, this unnamed, abused girl set out to rescue the nameless and abused girls of her day. Satan's plan to destroy her actually emboldened her resolve to help others. Her A21 Mission has offices around the world. They combat "human trafficking, establish prevention programs in schools and orphanages, represent victims as legal advocates, and give them refuge—in safe houses, then restoration in transition homes."[3] As of the writing of these words, several hundred young women have been assisted and released.[4]

Once again, what Satan intended for evil, God . . . Well, you know the rest.

Or do you? Do you believe that no evil is beyond God's reach?

That he can redeem every pit, including this one in which you find yourself?

What if Joseph had given up on God? Lord knows, he could have turned his back on heaven. At any point along his broken road, he could have turned sour and walked away. "No more. No more. I'm out."

You could give up on God as well. The cemetery of hope is over-populated with sour souls who have settled for a small god. Don't be among them.

God sees a Joseph in you. Yes, you! You in the pit. You with your family full of flops and failures. You incarcerated in your own version of an Egyptian jail. God is speaking to you.

Your family needs a Joseph, a courier of grace in a day of anger and revenge. Your descendants need a Joseph, a sturdy link in the chain of faith. Your generation needs a Joseph. There is a famine out there. Will you harvest hope and distribute it to the people? Will you be a Joseph?

Trust God. No, *really* trust him. He will get you through this. Will it be easy or quick? I hope so. But it seldom is. Yet God will make good out of this mess.

That's his job.

Questions
for Reflection

Prepared by CHRISTINE M. ANDERSON

you'll get through this

1. Three times at the beginning of the chapter, we read these lines: "You'll get through this. It won't be painless. It won't be quick. But God will use this mess for good. In the meantime don't be foolish or naive. But don't despair either. With God's help you will get through this."

   a. Consider each sentence one at a time. Which is most comforting or encouraging to you? Which, if any, do you wish Max *hadn't* included? Why?

   b. Max offers these words of assurance to three people in diverse situations: a woman with three children whose husband has left her, a middle-aged man fired for offensive comments, and a teenager forced to choose between her mother and father. How would you summarize in one sentence the difficult situation you face right now or one you have faced in the past?

   c. Max tells us three things not to do. Which negative word below do you relate to most? Which represents the greatest temptation for you now, or which is most characteristic of you when you are in a difficult situation?

   ❏ Foolish: I am tempted to be or have been thoughtless, reckless, shortsighted, lacking in wisdom and good judgment, or impulsive in my behavior.

   ❏ Naive: I am tempted to be or have been willfully ignorant of negative reality, lacking in discernment and critical judgment, blind to the impact of my words or behavior, or engaged in an unrealistic view of the world and human nature.

❑ Despairing: I am tempted to be or have been unwilling to receive comfort or care from others. I am prone to feel hopeless, desolate, despondent, helpless, or miserable.

❑ Other:

2. Read Genesis 37, which provides critical background about Joseph's family and details about his abduction and sale into slavery in Egypt.

a. The story features three primary characters: the brothers (as a whole), Joseph, and Jacob. Which of the "don't" words from question 1 best describes each of the three characters?

The brothers are _____.
Joseph is _____.
Jacob is _____.

b. Use the word you chose from question 1, and the character from Genesis 37 who best illustrates that word, to reflect on how you face difficulties. For example, if you chose "despairing," what similarities do you see between yourself and the despairing character you identified? What insights about your words, actions, or situation does this character provide? (You may wish to reread Genesis 37, paying particular attention to this character's words, actions, and situation.)

c. In what area, if any, do you resist being identified with this character? Why?

3. At the end of Genesis 37, Joseph finds himself in Egypt. The Hebrew word for Egypt is *Mitzrayim*, whose root means "to border, shut, or limit."[1] It evokes the image of a very narrow or tight place. We could say that Joseph's Egypt—his *Mitzrayim*—began the minute he was thrown into the pit. And the tight places kept coming—slavery, entrapment, prison.

   a. It would have been natural for Joseph to defy his captivity and devote all his efforts to escaping. Why do you suppose he repeatedly chose not to? What would you say he chose to do instead?

   b. How do you relate to this image of being in Egypt? How has your suffering hemmed you in or made your world much smaller than it once was? What limitations are most difficult for you?

   c. How would you characterize your response to your limitations? For example, are your thoughts and energies devoted primarily to escape plans, to ways to cope, or to something else?

4. Between the beginning and end of Joseph's story, he underwent a remarkable transformation. The spoiled youth who once thought of no one but himself became a visionary leader who saved the world from starvation. Every tight place in Joseph's life became a training place, a narrow path to an eternal purpose.

   a. Training is preparation. It is a process that makes the weak strong and the unskilled effective. What is the potential for training in your difficult situation? What new "muscles" are you working?

   b. Here is the assumption of training: what we can't do now even by trying very hard is something we will be able to do later by training very hard. How do you recognize this truth in both Joseph's story and your own?

5. "The story of Joseph is in the Bible for this reason: to teach you to trust God to trump evil. What Satan intends for evil, God, the Master Weaver and Master Builder, redeems for good" (p. 10). To *trump* is to get the better of an adversary by using a crucial, often hidden resource at the most strategic moment. How does this idea help you understand God's involvement in your life currently?

6. Author C. S. Lewis wrote, "God whispers to us in our pleasures, speaks in our conscience, but shouts in our pains."[2] Take a moment to reflect on what Joseph's story could reveal about the pain or difficulties you're experiencing. If God is shouting to you in your pain, what is he saying? How might he be inviting you to respond?

down, down, down to egypt

1. Joseph entered Egypt as a slave. He had lost everything, with one exception—his destiny. He believed that God was at work in his circumstances and had plans for his life.

   a. Overall, how would you describe the impact your circumstances have on your ability to trust God—to believe he is at work in your life?
   b. Reflect for a moment on the level of trust you have in God for your eternity—that he has saved you and that you will live with him forever. How does your level of trust in God for your eternity compare with your level of trust in God for your current circumstances? If your level of trust is higher for one than the other, what accounts for the difference?

2. One way to think about destiny is that we already know the ending of the story—God's and our own—and it is deeply good. Through the prophet Isaiah, God declares:

   > I am God, and there is none like me.
   > I make known the end from the beginning,
   >   from ancient times, what is still to come.
   > I say: My purpose will stand,
   >   and I will do all that I please. (46:9–10 NIV)

This kind of "mak[ing] known" reveals something utterly unique about who God is and how he works. We see a personal expression of this in Joseph's story when God used dreams to reveal what was to come (Gen. 37:5–11).

a. Recall a hardship or difficult season you experienced in the past. As you look back, what evidence was there of God's activity in your life? Unexpected kindnesses? Positive changes in circumstances or relationships? How did the hand of God prepare you for what followed? Did this season deepen your trust in God?

b. How do your previous experiences of God's work in your life—or his seeming absence—affect your ability to trust him in your current circumstances?

c. Think back over the last twenty-four hours. What signs of God's goodness and grace, however small, can you identify? Write down two or three.

d. What might those signs indicate about God's purposes in your life right now?

3. This is how we trust our destiny: we hold fast to what we have that we cannot lose. Max makes this practical by describing how people in two different circumstances—a job loss and a relationship loss—could remember and trust their destinies (pp. 18–19). Using the examples as a reference, write a two- to three-line statement that affirms your trust in the destiny God has for you.

4. "Survival in Egypt begins with a yes to God's call on your life" (p. 19). By saying yes, you acknowledge that nothing about you is unknown to God (Ps. 139). You affirm with David, "The LORD will work out his plans for my life—for your faithful love, O LORD, endures forever" (Ps. 138:8 NLT).

a. In what ways, if any, do you sense you might be saying no to God's call on your life?

b. If you considered that part of what you are saying no to is God's love, how would it change your perspective?

c. What yes might you say to God now, in this very moment?

alone but not all alone

Max offers four concrete ways we can open ourselves to the divine presence, which "surrounds us in the same way the Pacific surrounds an ocean floor pebble" (p. 27).

1. *Lay claim to the nearness of God.* The pages of Scripture are full of promises that affirm God's nearness to us:

> I may walk through valleys
> as dark as death,
>   but I won't be afraid.
> You are with me,
>   and your shepherd's rod
>   makes me feel safe. (Ps. 23:4 CEV)

> The LORD Almighty is here among us;
> the God of Israel is our fortress. (Ps. 46:7 NLT)

And be sure of this: I am with you always, even to the end of the age. (Matt. 28:20 NLT)

God has said,

> "Never will I leave you;
>   never will I forsake you." (Heb. 13:5 NIV)

When you lay claim to something, you assert your rights to it and demand it as due to you. It is a posture of boldness, insistence, and perseverance.

    a. How would you characterize your posture toward God's nearness? Have you been bold, insistent, and persistent in claiming this truth? Or have you tended to be more timid, passive, and ambivalent?

    b. "Difficult days demand decisions of faith" (p. 27). Using the passages above as a reference, personalize the promise of God's nearness by laying bold claim to it for the situation you face today. Write a two- or three-line statement asserting your decision to trust that God is near to you.

2. *Cling to his character.* The qualities of God are the unchanging aspects of his character; they are also promises we can rely on in the midst of change.

    a. Set a timer for two minutes. Write down as many truths about God's character as you can think of in that time. (Before setting the timer, you may wish to reread Max's list of God's qualities on p. 28.) Or if you are able to spend more time, read Psalm 86 and make a list of all God's qualities enumerated by David.

    b. Briefly review your list of God's qualities. Circle the two or three that stand out most to you. Why are these qualities especially important to you right now? What promises do they represent?

3. *Pray your pain out.* "Angry at God? Disappointed with his strategy? Ticked off at his choices? Let him know it. Let him have it! . . . Go ahead and file your grievance" (p. 29).

a. A grievance is a formal complaint about a problem or a wrong, filed by someone who has a right to be heard. Briefly identify the complaint you have about the difficulty you face now. What has gone wrong?

b. What emotions does this situation stir in you—about others, yourself, and God?

c. Speak plainly to God about your pain. You may choose to write your prayers in a journal or to speak them aloud. Resist the temptation to hide or withhold the truth about your thoughts and feelings. Bring the full weight of your hurts, questions, and disappointments to God.

4. *Lean on God's people.* God is present with those who gather in his name (Matt. 18:20). Max's vivid encouragement is to "be a barnacle on the boat of God's church" (p. 30). Barnacles begin life as tiny, free-swimming organisms, but they must attach themselves to a hard surface in order to grow into adulthood. To attach, they produce a kind of rubbery, liquid cement that eventually hardens. As barnacles mature, they continually produce concentric rings of cement, strengthening their attachment.

a. Overall, how would you characterize your current attachment to your faith community? Are you fully attached or still swimming free on your own? If attached, would you say your connection is growing weaker or stronger? Why?

b. Briefly reflect on specific relationships you have in your faith community—friends, a small group, a volunteer team you work with. Which relationship(s) would you say have the most "cement"?

c. When you lean on people, you depend on them. Which relationship(s) might you lean on more in the next week? How, specifically, will you depend on them? Ask for practical help? Solicit specific prayer? Meet for coffee to speak plain truth about what you're going through? Other possibilities?

stupid won't fix stupid

1. Navigating the demands of a "sandbar" crisis or a prolonged hardship can leave us depleted in many ways—mentally, emotionally, relationally, and spiritually. As you reflect on the demands you've had to navigate, how would you assess your level of depletion right now? Circle the number on the continuum that best describes your response.

1	2	3	4	5	6	7	8	9	10

I am depleted. I have little to no energy to engage in the tasks and relationships in my life.

I am not depleted. I have sufficient energy to engage in the tasks and relationships in my life.

   a. What image would you use to describe your level of depletion—a cloth worn thin, a dry riverbed, or a car running on fumes?
   b. What need(s) does your depletion image represent? In other words, what are you most aware of lacking right now?

2. Depletion can leave us vulnerable to what Max calls dumb becoming dumber, complicating our circumstances with things such as poor decisions, impulsive behavior, moral compromise, and more. Do you sense you're vulnerable because of your depletion? What resources can you tap in order to replenish yourself?

3. Justifications and rationalizations ("No one would know." "I won't get caught." "I'm only human.") are warning flags for dumb-becoming-dumber vulnerabilities. Author Dallas Willard wrote, "The most spiritually dangerous things in me are the little habits of thought, feeling, and action that I regard as 'normal' because 'everyone is like that' and it is 'only human.'"[3]

   a. What "little habits of thought, feeling, and action" are you aware of justifying or rationalizing?
   b. What potential dangers or harm could result from these vulnerabilities?

4. Read Genesis 39, which tells the story of Joseph's sandbar experience with Potiphar's wife.

   a. Justifications and rationalizations tend to keep our focus on what we lack and what's wrong with our circumstances. What does Joseph's response to his master's wife reveal about how he viewed his circumstances (v. 9)?
   b. Loyalty is faithfulness and devotion. What do you observe about loyalty—and disloyalty—in each of the characters in this chapter? Whom is each person trying to please? Consider the words and actions of Joseph, Potiphar, and Mrs. Potiphar.
   c. Using the three human characters in the chapter as a reference, how would you describe the object and extent of your loyalty right now? What do your words and actions reveal about whom you are trying to please?
   d. In what ways have you experienced God's loyalty—his faithfulness and devotion to you—in the midst of your circumstances?

5. Joseph placed his loyalty to God above everything else and refused to rationalize or justify a compromise. It was the right thing to do, but it was also costly.

   a. David wrote, "Do what is right as a sacrifice to the LORD and trust the LORD" (Ps. 4:5 NCV). What sacrifice might you have to make in connection with the vulnerabilities you identified in questions 2 and 3?

   b. What do you need to trust the Lord to handle?

oh, so this is boot camp!

1. "Every day God tests us through people, pain, or problems" (p. 61).

   a. When Max faced a test, he had to decide if he would pout or apologize, ignore the tension or deal with it. Think back over the last twenty-four hours, and identify a test that came your way. What was the choice or question you faced?

   b. In school some tests are graded, and others are pass/fail. How would you assess your response to the test you faced?

   c. The theme of Max's test might be described as relational integrity. What is the theme of the lesson your test represents? What gains could you realize if you learn this lesson well? What losses or consequences might you suffer if you fail to learn it?

2. God used the tests in Joseph's life—and he uses the tests in our lives—not as punishment but as preparation. It's a crucial distinction author C. S. Lewis affirmed when he wrote, "If you think of this world as a place intended simply for our happiness, you find it quite intolerable: think of it as a place of training and correction and it's not so bad."[4]

   a. What's your initial response to this idea? How does it affect your perspective on what it means to be tested by God?

   b. Joseph didn't know what his tests were preparing him for, but the lessons he learned were all about leadership, faithful service, and trust in God. Like Joseph, you may not know what God is preparing you for, but the lessons themselves might point in a certain direction. When you consider the lessons and themes of the tests you have experienced recently, where do you sense God may be leading you?

3. The biblical perspective on hardships is radically countercultural and counterintuitive. Here is how the author of James describes it:

> Consider it pure joy, my brothers, whenever you face trials of many kinds, because you know that the testing of your faith develops perseverance. Perseverance must finish its work so that you may be mature and complete, not lacking anything. (1:2–4 NIV)

a. The key to shifting our perspective on hardships begins with the two-word phrase "consider it." The Greek word for *consider* is a verb about thought, not emotion. "James is not commanding how one should *feel*, but rather how one should *think* about one's circumstances."[5] How do you respond to this distinction between thinking and feeling in connection with your circumstances? What concerns you or intrigues you about the idea of *thinking* joy even when you aren't feeling it?

b. One scholar suggests that instead of "looking *at* the trial," we look "*through* the trial to its potential outcome."[6] What words come to mind when you look *at* your trial? Similarly, what words come to mind when you look *through* your trial?

4. "Share the message God gives to you. This test will become your testimony . . . Your mess can become your message" (p. 52). In a court of law a testimony is an eyewitness's public declaration given under oath. It constitutes evidence in support of facts and

truth. What comes to mind when you think of yourself as an eyewitness to God's activity in the midst of your mess? What facts and truth about God are supported by the evidence of your testimony?

wait while God works

1. Joseph was probably seventeen when he was sold into slavery and thirty when Pharaoh put him in charge of famine preparations. His time of waiting—in Potiphar's house and in prison—spanned thirteen years.

   a. Take a moment to recall your age and the circumstances of your life thirteen years ago. Write down three things you remember about what that season of your life was like and then three things about your level of personal growth and maturity at the time. Consider spiritual, emotional, and relational maturity.

   b. What are some of the changes in your life and in your level of maturity between then and now?

   c. During Joseph's season of waiting and preparation, God was working. If you think about your last thirteen years as a similar time of waiting and preparation, how would you say God has been working in your circumstances and in your personal growth?

2. We are often in a hurry, but God is not. The pages of Scripture repeatedly encourage us to wait for the Lord. The psalmist provides a compelling image of what this kind of waiting looks like and what it requires:

With all my heart,
I am waiting, LORD, for you!
  I trust your promises.
I wait for you more eagerly
  than a soldier on guard duty
  waits for the dawn.
Yes, I wait more eagerly
  than a soldier on guard duty
  waits for the dawn.

Israel, trust the LORD!
  He is always merciful,
  and he has the power
  to save you. (Ps. 130:5–7 CEV)

The psalmist makes it clear that he has invested his whole heart in the expectation that the Lord is coming. Other Bible versions render the intensity of this longing for God as "I wait for the LORD, my soul waits" (NIV); "I am counting on the LORD; yes, I am counting on him" (NLT); "I pray to GOD—my life a prayer—and wait for what he'll say and do" (MSG).

a. When you consider the circumstances in which you are currently waiting on the Lord, how would you characterize the investment plan of your heart? Like the psalmist, are you 100 percent invested in waiting on the Lord? Or are you hedging your heart by also investing in things like worry or potential backup plans?

b. Using the various Bible versions previously quoted as references, write a statement that expresses the intensity of your longing for God right now.

    c. Overall, do you tend to be more aware of your longing for God or your longing for what you hope God will do for you? How do you distinguish between the two?

    d. How does the image of a soldier on night guard duty help you understand what it means to trust the Lord and to be active in your waiting?

3. "Waiting is a sustained effort to stay focused on God through *prayer* and *belief*. To wait is to '*rest* in the LORD, and wait patiently for Him . . .' (Ps. 37:7)" (p. 63, emphasis added). Use the sentence starters below to consider how you can actively wait on God in the days ahead.

    a. I can stay focused on God in *prayer* by . . .

    b. I can stay focused on God in my *beliefs* by . . .

    c. I can stay focused on God in *rest* by . . .

more bounce back than bozo

1. A ballast is a counterweight—a force that offsets an opposing force in order to maintain balance. Joseph's ballast was his "deep-seated, stabilizing belief in God's sovereignty" (p. 72). For thirteen years it helped him bounce back from every setback—betrayal, slavery, false accusations, imprisonment, abandonment. Joseph's audience with Pharaoh marked the beginning of his redemption, but there was still an opposing force at work. Only this time it wasn't a *setback*. It was a *setup*.

   a. Read Genesis 41:1–44, which tells the story of Pharaoh's dreams and his first encounter with Joseph. Pay particular attention to what Pharaoh said about Joseph (v. 15) and how Joseph responded (vv. 16, 25, 28, 32).

   b. A setup is a subtle invitation to self-deception, which in turn makes us vulnerable to a setback. How would you describe the potential setup in Pharaoh's words to Joseph (v. 15)? What kind of setbacks might Joseph have been vulnerable to later if he had accepted this subtle invitation?

   c. We see Joseph's ballast at work as he repeatedly affirmed God's sovereignty, not only in everything that had already happened (vv. 25, 28, 32), but also in describing what must happen next (vv. 16, 32). For Joseph, God's sovereignty covered both the past and the future.

   In this situation it would have been the most natural thing in the world for Joseph—who was just hours out of prison—to secure his future by putting the spotlight on himself. What does his refusal to do so reveal about his relationship with God? His trust in God's sovereignty?

d. Compare Pharaoh's statements in Genesis 41:15 and 41:39. How did Joseph's ballast impact Pharaoh's perspective? Consider what changed as well as what did not change.

2. The experience of moving from suffering to redemption is full of rich gifts and graces. Finally the long wait is over. There is relief, new life, new hope. But as Joseph's story shows, this transition also includes unique challenges.

a. As you anticipate or enter your own season of redemption, what setups—subtle invitations to self-deception—might you expect to encounter? Consider especially ways in which your focus might subtly shift from reliance on God to reliance on yourself.

b. What setbacks would you be vulnerable to if you accept these invitations? Consider especially the ways in which you might be tempted to secure your future on your own.

c. Joseph's ballast influenced Pharaoh's perspective. What significant relationships do you have that might be affected by how you handle your belief in God's sovereignty? How do you hope to influence their perspectives—about God and maybe even about you?

3. Bouncing back from a setback doesn't necessarily mean returning to life as it was. Joseph's redemption did not take him back to his old life in his father's house, and Lieutenant Sam Brown could never go back to the life he had before his horrific experience in

Afghanistan. For both men, bouncing back required two things: willingness to let go of what had been and openness to receive the new thing God offered. This is the promise of Scripture for everyone who perseveres:

God will bless you, if you don't give up when your faith is being tested. He will reward you with a glorious life, just as he rewards everyone who loves him. (James 1:12 CEV)

a. When you think of your hopes for redemption—what you want to be true when your season of waiting ends—to what degree are your hopes invested in going back to life as it was?

b. What thoughts or emotions arise when you consider that you may not go back to life as it was?

c. The reward for persevering—for loving God enough to make him your ballast—is a "glorious life." Another Bible version renders this promise: "For such persons loyally in love with God, the reward is life and more life" (MSG). It is a promise for eternal life, but it is also a promise for this life (Ps. 27:13–14).

In what areas do you sense God inviting you not merely to trust him more but to love him more?

What might you have to release in order to receive the new life God promises?

is God good when life isn't?

1. Christyn Taylor described how her one-way deal with God was shattered when she delivered a stillborn baby: "Fear set in, and my faith began to crumble. My 'safety zone' with God was no longer safe . . . anxiety began to overwhelm me" (p. 81).

   a. At some point in our journey, most of us have tried to offer God a contract. *I pledge to* _____ *if you, God, will* _____. What contractual agreements have you tried to make with God in the past? In your current circumstances?

   b. Christyn experienced a crisis of faith when God didn't meet her terms. How did the outcome of a past deal with God affect you? How did it affect your belief in God's goodness?

   c. In your current circumstances what questions do you find yourself asking about God? For example, If God could fix this, why doesn't he? How could a good God allow this? How could God bring good out of such evil?

2. "God promises to render beauty out of 'all things,' not 'each thing.' The isolated events may be evil, but the ultimate culmination is good" (p. 83).

   a. How do you respond to this distinction between "all things" and "each thing"? What light might it shed on your current circumstances or on the questions you asked in question 1c?

b. "We must let God define *good*" (p. 83). How do you imagine your life would be different if defining *good* were left to you? What potential advantages and disadvantages would you anticipate for the challenges you are facing?

3. The apostle Paul, who endured significant hardships and persecution, expected suffering to be part of a relationship with Christ:

> Everything God gives to his Son, Christ, is ours, too. But if we are to share his glory, we must also share his suffering. (Rom. 8:17 NLT)

> For you have been given not only the privilege of trusting in Christ but also the privilege of suffering for him. (Phil. 1:29 NLT)

Paul also emphasized the importance of having an eternal perspective:

> Yet what we suffer now is nothing compared to the glory he will give us later. (Rom. 8:18 NLT)

> Our present troubles are quite small and won't last very long. Yet they produce for us an immeasurably great glory that will last forever! (2 Cor. 4:17 NLT)

a. In human relationships we expect to share both the highs and the lows of life with those we love. How do your closest human relationships help you understand what it might mean for you to share in Christ's suffering as well as his glory?

b. We sometimes gain perspective on a problem by asking, *How much will this matter a week from now? A month from now?*

A year from now? Paul suggested that even a lifetime is too short to gain true perspective on our hardships; we need to view them from eternity.

Consider your current circumstances through all these time windows: a week from now, a month from now, a year from now, eternity. Think about the impact your difficulties have on such things as your daily life, your relationships, and your sense of well-being. In what ways, if any, does your perspective change over time?

4. After she lost her baby, Christyn Taylor wrestled with questions about why God had allowed it to happen. She wrote, "The only conclusion I came to was this: I have to give up my line in the sand. I have to offer my entire life, ever minute portion of it, to God's control regardless of the outcome" (p. 85).

   a. What comes to mind when you think of your lines in the sand—the things you are withholding from God's control?
   b. Surrendering control is always risky and often frightening, but is there anything about it that intrigues you or inspires hope in you? If you released everything to God, what might you experience that you couldn't experience any other way?

a splash of gratitude with that attitude, please

1. To incarnate is to take something that exists only as an idea or a theory and give it concrete form. In naming his sons, Joseph engaged in an incarnational act. He literally put a face—two faces!—on his gratitude.

   a. Recall a time you were overwhelmed with gratitude—to another human being or to God. How did you give concrete form to your gratitude? Consider your demeanor, your words, and your actions.

   b. Why was it important to you to express your gratitude in these ways? What might have been missed—by you and others—if you hadn't expressed your gratitude as you did?

   c. How does this particular experience of gratitude help you understand Joseph's act of gratitude in naming his two sons?

2. Naming in any form is a powerful act. Theologian Alexander Schmemann makes a connection between naming and gratitude:

   > To name a thing . . . is to bless God for it and in it. And in the Bible to bless God is not a "religious" . . . act, but the very *way of life*. God blessed the world, blessed man, blessed the seventh day (that is, time), and this means that He filled all that exists with His love and goodness . . . So [our] only *natural* . . . reaction . . . is to bless

God in return, to thank Him, to *see* the world as God sees it and—
in this act of gratitude and adoration—to know, name and possess
the world.[7]

a. A way of life is a daily experience—a composite of our routine
   attitudes, behaviors, and practices. Drawing on the experience
   of gratitude you identified in question 1, how would you
   describe what it means to make gratitude—blessing God—a
   way of life? What routine attitudes, behaviors, and practices
   would it require?
b. Gratitude requires seeing the world as God sees it. What do
   the names Joseph gave his sons (pp. 92–93) reveal about how
   he saw the world?

3. We can't *name*—express gratitude—until we *notice*. The practice
   of being thankful requires cultivating a posture of attentiveness
   that spotlights even the smallest graces.

a. Take a moment to get "small" in naming your gratitude. Write
   down two or three simple things you can thank God for—
   from the last twenty-four hours, the last hour, and this very
   moment.
b. How would you characterize your posture of attentiveness in
   your current season of life? In other words, to what degree do
   you routinely notice and name God's graces and gifts?

4. Max identified four potential reasons for failing to express
   gratitude. Place a check mark next to the reason(s) that come
   closest to describing your experience.

❏ Busyness: No time! I am so preoccupied with everything I have to do that I don't remember to express gratitude most of the time.

❏ Caution: Wait a second. This looks like a good thing, but I don't want to get my hopes up. It might be too good to be true. I'll keep my gratitude to myself until I know for sure.

❏ Self-centeredness: Okay, this is a good thing, and I'm grateful for it on one hand. But it requires something of me that I hadn't anticipated, so I have mixed feelings about it.

❏ Arrogance: Well, things weren't so bad before. And isn't all that sloppy gratitude just a sign of neediness? I'm not needy.

❏ Other:

Does this reason primarily characterize your expression of gratitude in your relationship with God, in your relationships with others, or in both?

What differences, if any, do you notice in your ability to express gratitude to *God* and to *others*? Do you express gratitude more frequently to one than the other? Are you more concrete in your gratitude to one than the other? More authentic? Describe the reasons for your response.

5. "In the midst of the darkest night of the human soul, Jesus found a way to give thanks. Anyone can thank God for the light. Jesus teaches us to thank God for the night" (p. 98). For what difficult aspect of your life do you sense God inviting you to express gratitude? Consider making your gratitude concrete, perhaps by writing it down, sharing it with someone, or marking it in another way. If you are not ready to express gratitude, express your concerns or reluctance to God instead. Ask for grace to take the next step.

now, about those family scandals and scoundrels

1. "[Joseph] kept family secrets a secret. Untouched and untreated. Joseph was content to leave his past in the past" (p. 102). Listed below are several words and phrases that characterize some of the hardships and dysfunction evident in Joseph's family. As you review the list, place a check mark next to any issues that have marked your family.

❏ Abandonment	❏ Betrayal
❏ Troubled marriage(s)	❏ Infertility
❏ Premature death	❏ Resentment
❏ Hatred	❏ Abuse
❏ Sibling rivalry	❏ Extramarital relationships
❏ Favoritism	❏ Harsh treatment
❏ Severe grief	❏ Brokenness
❏ Disregard for others	❏ Self-absorption
❏ Parental abdication	❏ Secrecy
❏ Guilt	❏ Neglect
❏ Deception	❏ Other:

a. Identify two or three long-term effects that these issues have had on you.

b. When you consider the hardships and dysfunction in your family, do you tend to feel as Joseph did, that it's better to leave these issues in the past? Or do you wish everything could be out in the open? How does your perspective compare with that of others in your family?

   c. What fears or concerns come to mind when you think about revisiting your family's past or talking with other family members about the long-term-impact issues you identified?

2. Part of the healing process includes unearthing the details—the specifics of how you were hurt—and inviting God to relive those experiences with you.

   a. What two or three details come to mind when you reflect on the long-term issues you identified in question 1? If you don't feel comfortable writing down the details, reflect instead on your resistance to doing so. What thoughts or emotions are you aware of when you consider writing down the specifics of what happened to you?

   b. As you consider your response to the previous question, what help do you need from God? How do you want to experience his presence, comfort, or guidance?

3. Coming face-to-face with old hurts can be disorienting. When Joseph first encountered his brothers again, he withheld his identity, spoke harshly, made false accusations, jailed them, released them, put conditions on their departure and return, held one of them hostage, concealed powerful emotions, and was secretly generous to them (Gen. 42:6–28).

   a. What conflicting thoughts and emotions surface when you consider the possibility of engaging old hurts and the people connected with them?

   b. Which of Joseph's behaviors do you relate to the most? Why?

4. "[God] gives us more than we request by going deeper than we

ask. He wants not only your whole heart; he wants your heart whole. Why? Hurt people hurt people" (p. 105).

    a. In what area of your life do you most feel as if your heart is not whole? It might be in a difficult relationship, personal insecurities, a significant loss, self-defeating behaviors, or a pattern of sin or failure. Briefly summarize the situation.

    b. What is the specific hole in your heart related to the area you identified? For example, if you identified a difficult relationship, the hole in your heart might be an inability to forgive, lack of hope for reconciliation, or grief over the past.

    c. How might this lack of heart wholeness have led you to say or do things that hurt or negatively affected someone? Consider past relationships as well as recent relationships.

5. Joseph's path to reconciliation with his family was long and difficult, but it began with a small act of mercy and grace—he loaded his brothers' saddlebags with grain and quietly returned the silver they had paid for it. A gift, free and clear.

    a. Joseph gave his brothers what they needed most. They were prepared to pay for it, but he gave it as a gift. What do you think your family members need most from you in connection with the past?

    b. What small act of mercy and grace do you sense God inviting you to extend to someone in your family?

revenge feels good, but then . . .

1. Revenge is retaliation—an attempt to even the scales of justice by punishing someone who wronged us. In some cases, such as Joseph Richardson's Spite House, retaliation can be extreme.

   a. Like Richardson, some people retaliate by striking out in hostile ways. Others express their hostility by striking *in*; they withdraw emotionally or even sever the relationship. Which approach—striking out or striking in—best describes your tendency?

   b. Identify one or two subtle or not-so-subtle ways you have taken revenge on someone who hurt you. How did your actions affect the other person? How did they affect you?

2. The apostle Peter addressed the issue of revenge by putting it in the context of our relationship with Christ:

   Christ suffered for you, leaving you an example, that you should follow in his steps . . . When they hurled their insults at him, he did not retaliate; when he suffered, he made no threats. Instead, he entrusted himself to him who judges justly. (1 Peter 2:21, 23 NIV)

   a. The Greek word translated as "entrusted" is *paradidōmi* (par-ad-id´-o-mee). It means "to hand over or deliver into someone else's custody." In ancient Greece it was used to describe handing over a captive or delivering a prisoner to court.[8] Using these images as a reference, how would you describe what it means to entrust oneself to God instead of taking revenge?

b. Reflect on what you have read about Joseph's encounters with his brothers, and identify ways Joseph entrusted himself and what he suffered to God.

c. How does this passage challenge you or encourage you concerning your suffering or desire for revenge?

3. "Fix your enemies? That's God's job. Forgive your enemies? Ah, that's where you and I come in" (p. 116). As believers, we are to go well beyond not taking revenge; the command is to love our enemies:

You're familiar with the old written law, "Love your friend," and its unwritten companion, "Hate your enemy." I'm challenging that. I'm telling you to love your enemies. Let them bring out the best in you, not the worst. When someone gives you a hard time, respond with the energies of prayer, for then you are working out of your true selves, your God-created selves. This is what God does. He gives his best—the sun to warm and the rain to nourish—to everyone, regardless: the good and bad, the nice and nasty. (Matt. 5:43–45 MSG)

a. What characteristics are true of you when you are at your best? Write down no more than five words or phrases. For example, you might say something like, "I am kind, generous, resourceful."

b. What comes to mind when you consider giving your best— your God-created self—to the people you need to forgive or you find difficult to love?

4. "Forgiveness vacillates like this. It has fits and starts, good days and bad . . . But this is okay. When it comes to forgiveness, all of us are beginners. . . . As long as you are trying to forgive, you are forgiving" (p. 117).

   a. Briefly reflect on efforts you have made to forgive someone. How did you approach it? Did you feel as if you had to make a one-time decision? Did you move into it gradually? Did the process have fits and starts?
   b. How would assess yourself now regarding forgiveness? Would you say you are actively trying to forgive or actively avoiding it?
   c. Jesus' directive in the Matthew 5 passage is to "respond with the energies of prayer." How might you pray specifically for the benefit and blessing of the person who hurt you?

CHAPTER 12

the prince is your brother

1. "Big brothers can make all the difference" (p. 122).

   a. In your opinion what are the defining characteristics of the ideal big brother (or sister)? Write down a few words or phrases.

   b. What were your big-brother needs when you were growing up? In what situations did you most need someone who embodied the characteristics you just wrote down?

   c. In these situations how did having—or not having—a protector affect you?

   d. What are your big-brother needs now? When do you most often wish someone would be there for you in the ways you identified above?

2. Joseph and his brothers shared a dramatic and tender reunion (pp. 123–24).

   a. As you read the story, in what ways did you identify with Joseph, who was in a position of strength and had to choose whether or not to forgive?

   b. In what ways did you identify with the brothers, who were vulnerable, depleted, and in need of forgiveness?

   c. Read Genesis 45:1–15. What big-brother characteristics do you recognize in Joseph's treatment of his brothers?

3. The apostle Paul provided a compelling image of Christ as a brother:

> For God knew his people in advance, and he chose them to become like his Son, so that his Son would be the firstborn, with many brothers and sisters . . .
>
> Who then will condemn us? Will Christ Jesus? No, for he is the one who died for us and was raised to life for us and is sitting at the place of highest honor next to God, pleading for us. (Rom. 8:29, 34 NLT)

Consider the last line of this passage again, this time from *The Message*:

> The One who died for us—who was raised to life for us!—is in the presence of God at this very moment sticking up for us. (v. 34)

a. The Bible includes many metaphors for Christ, including a shepherd (John 10:11), a vine (15:5), light (8:12), and bread (6:35). What unique insights does the image of Christ as a brother—especially a firstborn—provide about who he is?

b. In what ways, if any, have you experienced Christ as someone who cares for you as an ideal big brother would (refer back to question 1)?

c. How do you need Jesus to stick up for you, to plead for you in the circumstances you face now?

4. "You will get through this. Not because you are strong but because your Brother is. Not because you are good but because your Brother is" (p. 128).

a. In your current circumstances how do you tend to rely more on your own strengths or try very hard to be "good" in order to get through it?

b. What makes it difficult for you to rely on Christ for these things and to trust him to help you get through it in his way?

good-bye to good-byes

1. "Death is the most difficult good-bye of all" (p. 132).

   a. To whom have you had to say a final good-bye? What additional losses deepened your grief after this person's death? The loss of hopes or plans for the future, companionship, holidays together?

   b. Even if we haven't lost a loved one to death, suffering always includes some kind of loss. What losses have you incurred in the difficulties you're currently facing? The loss of security, a relationship, opportunity, employment, freedom, health, dreams?

2. "The rest of the world has moved on; you ache to do the same. But you can't; you can't say good-bye" (p. 135). Sometimes we refuse to say good-bye because doing so requires finally accepting that someone or something we love is irretrievably lost to us.

   a. Of the losses you wrote down in question 1, which would you say you have yet to fully grieve and let go of?

   b. What makes it especially difficult for you to say good-bye?

3. Take a few moments to immerse yourself in biblical truths about heaven. As you read through the following passages in your Bible, write down the words or phrases that stand out to you.

Revelation 21:3–4

2 Corinthians 5:1–5

John 14:1–3

Philippians 3:20–21

1 Corinthians 15:50–54

Revelation 22:3–5

Psalm 16:11

1 John 3:2

Luke 22:28–30

a. Briefly review the words and phrases you wrote down. What connections do you make between your words and phrases and the losses you identified in question 1?

b. What comfort or reassurance did you find in those verses?

4. Author C. S. Lewis wrote:

Both good and evil, when they are full grown, become retrospective . . . That is what mortals misunderstand. They say of some temporal suffering, "No future bliss can make up for it," not knowing that Heaven, once attained, will work backwards and turn even that agony into a glory.[9]

a. How do you respond to the idea that good grows—that it begins in an immature state and eventually becomes "full grown"? In what ways does it affirm or challenge your experiences?

b. Knowing that some things will reach their fully grown goodness only in heaven, how would you assess the development of goodness in your current losses or difficulties? Is it still hidden like a seed underground? Just beginning to sprout? Actively growing and bearing fruit?

c. What comes to mind when you think of heaven as "retrospective," working backward in your life? What is the first thing you hope will be transformed into glory?

5. The writer of Hebrews invites us to see ourselves as athletes in the stadium on race day (12:1–3). Imagine . . . as you circle another lap on the track in your long-distance race, the roar of cheers and encouragement from the crowd is nearly deafening. And your encouragers are not mere spectators but decorated athletes; they know what it takes not only to finish the race but to win it. These are among your biggest fans—Abraham, Sarah, Isaac, Jacob, Joseph, and all who have finished their races ahead of you (chap. 11). All the people in the stadium are on their feet. Everyone is cheering you on: "Run! Run! Run!"

a. As you run your race, whose faces do you want to see in the crowd of witnesses surrounding you? Consider biblical characters who are meaningful to you as well as loved ones who have finished their races ahead of you.

b. What do you most need to hear from the people you see in your cheering crowd? What encouragement will help you keep running, fixing your eyes on Jesus and the joy set before you?

keep calm and carry on

1. Joseph assumed God was in his crisis. "God preceded the famine. God would outlive the famine. God was all over the famine" (p. 145).

   a. To what degree do you believe God is at work in the difficulties you face right now? Is your level of belief very low, moderate, high? How would you describe it?
   b. What two or three factors most influenced your assessment? Factors might include past or recent events, experiences, relationships, beliefs.

2. Max presented two stories about how God took something initially painful and used it for something extremely good (pp. 146–47).

   a. In your current difficulties what pain do you hope God will put to use for something good?
   b. If you could know for certain that God would put your pain to use, how do you imagine it would change your current experience?

3. In the race to the South Pole, Roald Amundsen followed a plan of progressing fifteen to twenty miles a day regardless of the weather; Robert Scott followed no set plan, driving too hard on good days and stopping on bad days. In a book he later published

about the race, Amundsen wrote, "Victory awaits him who has everything in order—luck, people call it. Defeat is certain for him who has neglected to take the necessary precautions in time; this is called bad luck."[10]

a. What similarities do you recognize between Amundsen's strategy and philosophy in conquering the hazards of the South Pole and Joseph's approach in conquering the crisis of the famine?

b. What do you think it means to "take the necessary precautions in time" when navigating a personal challenge or crisis? For reference, you might consider how Joseph did this not only when he had the power and authority to manage the famine but also how he did it when he was a servant in Potiphar's house and an inmate in prison.

c. Would you say you tend to be more like Scott, allowing good days and bad days to dictate your response, or more like Amundsen, making steady progress regardless of circumstances?

d. How does the story of the two men challenge you about your situation? How does it encourage you?

4. Management experts Jim Collins and Morten Hansen identified self-control as the primary distinguishing characteristic of corporate leaders who succeed in turbulent times (p. 149). Author Dallas Willard defines self-control as "the steady capacity to direct yourself to accomplish what you have chosen or decided to do and be, even though you 'don't feel like it.'"[11]

a. As you consider the crises or challenges you face, where do you tend to lack confidence in your ability to exercise self-control? What factors make it especially difficult for you?

b. The promise of Scripture is that "God is working in you, giving you the desire to obey him and the power to do what pleases him" (Phil. 2:13 NLT). What desire and power do you need from God in order to resist the "I don't feel like it" impulse?

5. "You can map out a strategy. Remember, God is in this crisis. Ask him to give you an index card–sized plan, two or three steps you can take today" (p. 149).

a. Depending on where you are in your crisis or difficulty, a plan might be as short-term as how to navigate the demands of the next hour or as long-term as laying out weeks or months in advance. What time frame do you feel comfortable planning for right now? An hour, a day, a week, or longer?

b. What do you want to achieve in that time frame? Try to keep your goal specific and measurable. For example, "trust God more" is a good thing to do but a difficult goal to measure. A more measurable goal could be "Every time I feel afraid, I will entrust myself to God by writing a brief prayer in my journal."

c. What two or three steps can you take to progress toward your goal? If you need help to identify or follow through on the next steps, whom might you contact for help?

evil. God. good.

1. Listed below are ten biblical truths you've explored throughout *You'll Get Through This*.

   - Nothing in my life is unknown to God (Ps. 139).
   - God is near to me (Ps. 23:4).
   - The Lord will work out his plans for my life (Ps. 138:8).
   - God uses experiences of testing to train and prepare me (James 1:2–4); all tests are temporary (1 Peter 1:6).
   - God is always at work in me (Phil. 1:6).
   - I can wait for the Lord because he is faithful, merciful, and powerful (Ps. 130:5–7).
   - The reward for perseverance is a glorious life (James 1:12).
   - An eternal perspective puts my troubles in perspective (2 Cor. 4:17).
   - Jesus advocates for me (Rom. 8:34).
   - In God's hands intended evil becomes eventual good (Gen. 50:20).

   a. How have these truths affected your view or experience of the challenges of life? In what ways, if any, would you say this represents a shift from where you were at the beginning of the book?

   b. Which two or three truths are most important to you right now? What need(s) do these truths meet?

   c. Write a statement personalizing one or more of the truths that are important to you. For example: God already knows what I will face tomorrow. No evil in my life will prevent God from working out his plans for me. God is near to me when I am lonely. My suffering is not meaningless—God can use it to train me, and God will use it for good.

d. Consider how you might make your personal statement a concrete reminder of God's faithfulness to you. You could share it with two or three friends and ask them to e-mail or text it to you throughout the week. Memorize the scripture your statement is based on, or post it where you will see it daily. Print your statement on a small card, and attach the card to a potted plant as a visual reminder that your faith is growing even in this difficult season.

2. "When God gets in the middle of life, evil becomes good" (p. 155).

a. Make a simple, three-column chart on a piece of paper. Beginning with the first column on the left, title the columns Evil, God, and Good.

b. In the first column write down two or three phrases with specifics about the challenge you're experiencing.

c. In the second column prayerfully record details of God's character that are relevant to this challenge.

d. In the third column reflect on any good that has come from God's activity in your situation. If you struggle to identify anything good, consider the good you hope will eventually come from what you are going through. An example follows.

Evil	God	Good
I lost my job.	God is generous, sovereign, and always near. Changes do not baffle or intimidate him.	I no longer attach my sense of security to my job. My security is in God's hands.

3. Max shares Christine Caine's story (pp. 157–58) to demonstrate how God can use our darkness to spread light.

   a. As you reflect on what you wrote on your chart, what "light" do you sense God may be inviting you to spread?
   b. Responding to God's invitation doesn't require figuring everything out at once; it requires only taking the next step, however small it might be. What one simple step could you take within the next twenty-four hours to respond to God's invitation?

4. Chapter 1 sets up the message of the book by emphasizing this encouraging statement: "You'll get through this. It won't be painless. It won't be quick. But God will use this mess for good. In the meantime don't be foolish or naive. But don't despair either. With God's help you will get through this."

   a. Briefly reflect on the personal journey you've taken as you read this book. Consider especially any ways in which you have experienced God's care for you (in comfort, encouragement, wisdom, provision, perseverance).
   b. How is God's care for you helping you "get through this"?
   c. Set aside time for quiet prayer. Express your gratitude to God for all the ways he has demonstrated his care for you. Entrust your ongoing questions and struggles to him, and ask him for what you need right now. Allow a few moments of quiet, inviting God to speak his words of love to you in the silence. Close your time by praising God for who he is and for his sovereignty in your life.

Notes

Chapter 1: You'll Get Through This

1. Emphasis mine.
2. Spiros Zodhiates, ed., *The Hebrew-Greek Key Word Study Bible: Key Insights into God's Word, New American Standard Bible*, rev. ed. (Chattanooga, TN: AMG, 2008), Genesis 50:20. See also "Greek/Hebrew Definitions," Bible Tools, Strong's #2803, *chashab*, www.bibletools.org/index.cfm/fuseaction/Lexicon.show/ID/H2803 /chashab.htm.
3. The same term is used in Genesis 13:4 ("he had . . . *built* an altar" [NIV]), Job 9:9 ("He *made* the Bear"), and Proverbs 8:26 ("he *made* the earth" [NIV]).
4. Zodhiates, *The Hebrew-Greek Key Word Study Bible*, Genesis 50:20. See also *Strong's Exhaustive Bible Concordance Online*, #6213, www.biblestudytools.com/lexicons/hebrew/nas/asah.html.
5. Genesis 50:20 is from *The Message*.
6. Emphasis mine.
7. Joseph was probably seventeen when he was sold to the Midianites (Gen. 37:2). He was twenty-eight when the butler, who promised to help him get out of prison, was released (40:21–23). Two years later, when Joseph was thirty, Joseph interpreted Pharaoh's dreams (41:1, 46). And Joseph was about thirty-nine when his brothers came to Egypt the second time (45:1–6), in the second year of the famine following the seven years of plenty.

Chapter 2: Down, Down, Down to Egypt

1. "Every shepherd is an abomination to the Egyptians" (Gen. 46:34).

Chapter 3: Alone but Not All Alone

1. JJ Jasper, personal conversations with the author. Used by permission.
2. Thomas Lye, "How Are We to Live by Faith on Divine Providence?" in *Puritan Sermons 1659–1689* (Wheaton, IL: Richard Owen Roberts, Publisher, 1981), 1:378.
3. Emphasis mine.
4. Emphasis mine.
5. Edward Mote, "The Solid Rock," in *Sacred Selections for the Church*, comp. and ed. Ellis J. Crum (Kendallville, IN: Sacred Selections, 1960), 120.
6. Augustine, *Saint Augustine: Sermons on the Liturgical Seasons*, trans. Sister Mary Sarah Muldowney (New York: Fathers of the Church, 1959), 85–86.
7. Emphasis mine.

Chapter 4: Stupid Won't Fix Stupid

1. Genesis 39:5.
2. David M. Edwards, "Song Story; Take My Hand, Precious Lord: The Life of Thomas Dorsey," *Worship Leader Magazine*, March/April 2010, 64–65. Copyright © 2010 by Worship Leader Partnership. Used by permission. All rights reserved.
3. Ibid, 65.
4. Thomas A. Dorsey, "Take My Hand, Precious Lord" (Hialeah, FL: Warner-Tamerlane, 1938, renewed). All rights reserved. Used by permission.
5. Edwards, "Song Story," 65.

Chapter 5: Oh, So This Is Boot Camp!

1. Howard Rutledge and Phyllis Rutledge with Mel White and Lyla White, *In the Presence of Mine Enemies—1965–1973: A Prisoner of War* (New York: Fleming H. Revell, 1975), 33, 35.
2. Emphasis mine.
3. Spiros Zodhiates, ed., *The Hebrew-Greek Key Word Study Bible: Key Insights into God's Word, New American Standard Bible*, rev. ed. (Chattanooga, TN: AMG, 2008), #977, p. 1817. See also *Strong's Concordance with Hebrew and Greek Lexicon*, http://www.eliyah.com/cgi-bin/strongs.cgi?file=hebrewlexicon&isindex=977.

4. Emphasis mine.
5. Bob Benson, *"See You at the House.": The Stories Bob Benson Used to Tell* (Nashville: Generoux, 1986), 202–3.
6. Rutledge and Rutledge, *In the Presence*, 39, 52.

Chapter 6: Wait While God Works

1. Psalm 46:10.

Chapter 7: More Bounce Back Than Bozo

1. Jay Kirk, "Burning Man," GQ.com, February 2012, www.gq.com /news-politics/newsmakers/201202/burning-man-sam-brown-jay-kirk -gq-february-2012, 108–15; Sam Brown, personal conversation with the author. Used by permission.

Chapter 8: Is God Good When Life Isn't?

1. Christyn Taylor, CaringBridge.org, August 22, 2010, created at http:// www.caringbridge.org/visit/rebeccataylor1. Used by permission.
2. Joni Eareckson Tada, "God's Plan A," in *Be Still, My Soul: Embracing God's Purpose and Provision in Suffering*, ed. Nancy Guthrie (Wheaton, IL: Crossway, 2010), 32–33, 34.
3. Donald G. Bloesch, *The Struggle of Prayer* (Colorado Springs, CO: Helmers and Howard, 1988), 33.
4. Taylor, CaringBridge.

Chapter 9: A Splash of Gratitude with That Attitude, Please

1. Henry Ward Beecher, *Proverbs from Plymouth Pulpit: Selected from the Writings and Sayings of Henry Ward Beecher*, comp. William Drysdale (New York: D. Appleton, 1887), 13.
2. Special thanks to Daniel for allowing me to share his story.

Chapter 10: Now, About Those Family Scandals and Scoundrels

1. Genesis 37:2.
2. Genesis 43:30; 45:2, 14, 15; 46:29; 50:1, 17.

Chapter 11: Revenge Feels Good, but Then . . .

1. "Spite House," New York Architecture Images, nyc-architecture.com, http://nyc-architecture.com/GON/GON005.htm.
2. *Strong's Exhaustive Bible Concordance Online*, #5117, www.biblestudytools.com/lexicons/greek/nas/topos.html.

Chapter 12: The Prince Is Your Brother

1. Rick Reilly, "Matt Steven Can't See the Hoop. But He'll Still Take the Last Shot," Life of Reilly, ESPN.com, March 11, 2009, http://sports.espn.go.com/espnmag/story?id=3967807. See also Gil Spencer, "Blind Player Helps Team See the Value of Sportsmanship," *Delaware County Daily Times*, February 25, 2009, www.delcotimes.com/articles/2009/02/25/sports/doc49a4c50632d09134430615.

2. In retaliation for an attack on their sister, Simeon and Levi slaughtered all the males in the village of Shechem (Genesis 34).

3. Emphasis mine.

Chapter 13: Good-bye to Good-byes

1. "John Herschel Glenn, Jr. (Colonel, USMC, Ret.) NASA Astronaut (Former)," National Aeronautics and Space Administration, Biographical Data, www.jsc.nasa.gov/bios/htmlbios/glenn-j.html.

2. Bob Greene, "John Glenn's True Hero," CNN.com, February 20, 2012, www.cnn.com/2012/02/19/opinion/greene-john-annie-glenn/index.html.

3. From a conversation with Steven Chapman on November 30, 2011. Used by permission.

4. Todd Burpo with Lynn Vincent, *Heaven Is for Real: A Little Boy's Astounding Story of His Trip to Heaven and Back* (Nashville: Thomas Nelson, 2011), 94–96.

Chapter 14: Keep Calm and Carry On

1. "The Story of Keep Calm and Carry On," YouTube video, 3:01, posted by Temujin Doran, www.youtube.com/watch?v=FrHkKXFRbCI&sns=fb. See also *Keep Calm and Carry On: Good Advice for Hard Times* (Kansas City, MO: Andrews McMeel, 2009), introduction.

2. Jim Collins, "How to Manage Through Chaos," CNN Money, September 30, 2011, http://management.fortune.cnn.com/2011/09/30/jim-collins-great-by-choice-exclusive-excerpt.

3. Ibid.

Chapter 15: Evil. God. Good.

1. Christine Caine, *Undaunted: Daring to Do What God Calls You to Do* (Grand Rapids: Zondervan, 2012), 48.

2. Ibid., 48–49.

3. Ibid., 191.

4. Christine Caine, personal communication with the author, October 8, 2012.

Questions for Reflection

1. Francis Brown, S. R. Driver, Charles A. Briggs, *Brown-Driver-Briggs Hebrew and English Lexicon* (Peabody, MA: Hendrickson, 1996), 595–96.
2. C. S. Lewis, *The Problem of Pain* (New York: Macmillan, 1962), 93.
3. Dallas Willard, *The Divine Conspiracy: Rediscovering Our Hidden Life in God* (San Francisco: HarperSanFrancisco, 1998), 344.
4. C. S. Lewis, *God in the Dock* (Grand Rapids: Wm. B. Eerdmans, 1970), 52.
5. Craig L. Blomberg and Mariam J. Kamell, *James*, vol. 16 of *Zondervan Exegetical Commentary on the New Testament*, gen. ed. Clinton E. Arnold (Grand Rapids: Zondervan, 2008), 49.
6. Scot McKnight, *The Letter of James*, The New International Commentary on the New Testament (Grand Rapids: Wm. B. Eerdmans, 2011), 71.
7. Alexander Schmemann, *For the Life of the World: Sacraments and Orthodoxy* (Crestwood, NY: St. Vladimir's Seminary Press, 1973), 15.
8. Hartmut Beck, *New International Dictionary of New Testament Theology*, vol. 2, gen. ed., Colin Brown (Grand Rapids: Zondervan, 1986), "paradidōmi."
9. C. S. Lewis, *The Great Divorce* (New York: Macmillan, 1946), 67.
10. Roald Amundsen, *The South Pole* (Seattle: CreateSpace Independent Publishing Platform, 2012), 139.
11. Dallas Willard, *Renovation of the Heart: Putting on the Character of Christ* (Colorado Springs: NavPress, 2002), 127.

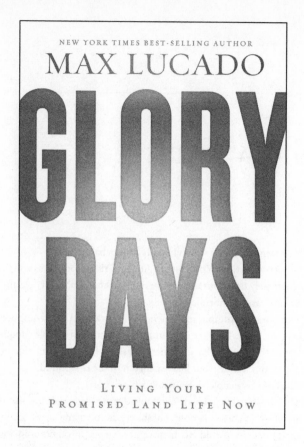

NEW YORK TIMES BEST-SELLING AUTHOR

MAX LUCADO

GLORY DAYS

LIVING YOUR
PROMISED LAND LIFE NOW

Enjoy this excerpt of Max's book, *Glory Days*.

1

Glory Days

For seven years they were virtually untouchable.

Seven nations conquered. At least thirty-one kings defeated. Approximately ten thousand square miles of choice property claimed.

Seven years of unbridled success.

They were outnumbered but not outpowered. Underequipped but not overwhelmed. They were the unlikely but unquestionable conquerors of some of the most barbaric armies in history. Had the campaign been a prizefight, the referee would have called it in the first round.

The Hebrew people were unstoppable.[1]

They hadn't always been. The Bible doesn't gloss over the checkered history of God's chosen people. Abraham had too many wives. Jacob told too many lies. Esau sold his birthright. Joseph's brothers sold Joseph.

---

1. "Conquest Confusion at Yale," Bryant G. Wood, BibleArcheology.org, November 20, 2012, www.biblearchaeology.org/post/2012/11/20/Conquest-Confusion-at-Yale. aspx#Article. Also see, Ronald B. Allen, "The Land of Israel," in *Israel: The Land and the People: An Evangelical Affirmation of God's Promises*, ed. H. Wayne House (Grand Rapids, MI: Kregel Publications, 1998), 17–18, 24. Caleb says he was forty years old when he went to spy out Canaan (Josh. 14:7). The Hebrews were in the wilderness for forty years (Ex. 16:35). They wandered in the wilderness for thirty-eight years after the spies returned, which means Caleb was seventy-eight years old at the beginning of the conquest. Caleb says he is eighty-five years old in Joshua 14:10, forty-five years of grace from God since Kadesh Barnea (38+7).

Four centuries of Egyptian bondage were followed by forty years of wilderness wandering. Then later, seventy years of Babylonian detention.

The Hebrew people built two temples only to lose them. They were given the ark of the covenant only to lose it. Babylonia built her cities. Greece flexed her muscles. Rome stretched her empire. And Israel? In the schoolroom of ancient societies, she was the kid with the black eye, bullied and beat-up.

Except for those seven years. The Glory Days of Israel. On the time line of your Bible, the era glistens between the difficult days of Exodus and the dark age of the judges. Moses had just died, and the Hebrews were beginning their fifth decade as bedouin in the badlands. And sometime around 1400 BC,[2] God spoke, Joshua listened, and the Glory Days began. The Jordan River opened up. The Jericho walls fell down. The sun stood still, and the kings of Canaan were forced into early retirement. Evil was booted and hope rebooted. By the end of the campaign, the homeless wanderers became hope-filled homesteaders. A nation of shepherds began to quarry a future out of the Canaanite hills. They built farms, villages, and vineyards. The accomplishments were so complete that the historian wrote:

> So the Lord gave to Israel all the land of which He had sworn to give to their fathers, and they took possession of it and dwelt in it. The Lord gave them rest all around, according to all that He had sworn to their fathers. And not a man of all their enemies stood against them; the Lord delivered all their enemies into their hand. Not a word failed of any good thing which the Lord had spoken to the house of Israel. All came to pass. (Josh. 21:43–45)

What sweeping statements! "The Lord gave . . . all the land." "The Lord gave them rest." "Not a man of all their enemies stood against them." "All came to pass." Winter chill gave way to springtime thaw, and a new season was born.

Perhaps you need a new season as well. You don't need to cross the

---

2. Kenneth O. Gangel, *Holman Old Testament Commentary: Joshua,* ed. Max Anders (Nashville, TN: B&H, 2002), 2.

Jordan River, but you need to get through the week. You aren't facing Jericho, but you are facing rejection or heartache. Canaanites don't stalk you, but disease, discouragement, danger? Rampant. You wonder if you have what it takes to face tomorrow.

You can relate to the deflated little fellow I saw in an airport terminal. He and his family were on summer vacation. At least that's what I Sherlocked from the way they were dressed. Flip-flops, baseball caps, and straw hats. They were beach-bound for a week of sand and sun.

Everything about the dad's expression said, "Hurry up! We have to run if we are going to make the connection!" The concourse was his football field and the departure gate his end zone. He was determined to score a touchdown.

Can the little fellow keep up? I wondered. Mom could. She matched her husband stride for stride. The big brothers could. They hitched their backpacks higher and leaned forward into the draft of their parents.

But the little guy? He was five years old, six at most. His face was resolved, but his legs were so short. It didn't help matters that he was dragging a pint-size Mickey Mouse carry-on bag. Nor did it help that the entire civilized world was jammed into the airport. He tried to match his parents' pace, but he just couldn't.

So he stopped. Right in the middle of the mayhem, he gave up. He plopped his bag on the floor, sat on top of it, and shouted in the direction of his disappearing family, "I can't keep up!"

Can you relate?

Sometimes the challenge is just too much. You want to keep up. You try. It's not that you don't. You just run out of fight. Life has a way of taking the life out of us.

The book of Joshua is in the Bible for such seasons. It dares us to believe our best days are ahead of us. God has a Promised Land for us to take.

The Promised Land was the third stop on the Hebrews' iconic itinerary. Their pilgrimage began in Egypt, continued through the wilderness, and concluded in Canaan. Each land represents a different condition of life. Geography is theology. In Egypt the Hebrews were enslaved to Pharaoh. In the wilderness they were free from Pharaoh but still enslaved to fear. They refused to enter the Promised Land and languished in the desert. Only in Canaan did they discover victory. Egypt, the wilderness, and Canaan. Slaves to Pharaoh, slaves to fear, and, finally, people of the promise.

We, too, have traveled this itinerary. Egypt represents our days before salvation. We were in bondage to sin. We wore the leg irons of guilt and death. But then came our Deliverer, Jesus Christ. By his grace and in his power, we crossed the Red Sea. He liberated us from the old life and offered a brand-new life in Canaan.

Our Promised Land isn't a physical territory; it is a spiritual reality. It's not real estate but a real state of the heart and mind.

A Promised Land life in which "we are more than conquerors through [Christ] who loved us" (Rom. 8:37).

A life in which "we do not lose heart" (2 Cor. 4:16).

A life in which "[Christ's] love has the first and last word in everything we do" (2 Cor. 5:14 MSG).

A life in which we are "exceedingly joyful in all our tribulation" (2 Cor. 7:4).

A life in which we are "anxious for nothing" (Phil. 4:6), in which we are "praying always" (Eph. 6:18), in which we "do all in the name of the Lord Jesus, giving thanks to God the Father through Him" (Col. 3:17).

Canaan is a life defined by grace, refined by challenge, and aligned with a heavenly call. In God's plan, in God's *land*, we win more often than we lose, forgive as quickly as we are offended, and give as abundantly as we receive. We serve out of our giftedness and delight in our assignments. We may stumble, but we do not collapse. We may struggle, but we defy despair. We boast only in Christ, trust only in God, lean wholly on his power. We enjoy abundant fruit and increasing faith.

Canaan symbolizes the victory we can have today. In spite of what the hymn suggests—"To Canaan's land I'm on my way, where the soul of man never dies"[3]—Canaan is not a metaphor for heaven. The idea is beautiful, but the symbolism doesn't work. Heaven will have no enemies; Canaan

3. "To Canaan's Land I'm on My Way," *Praise for the Lord* (Nashville, TN: Praise Press, 1992), 694.

had at least seven enemy nations. Heaven will have no battles. Joshua and his men fought at least thirty-one (Josh. 12:9–24). Heaven will be free of stumbles and struggle. Joshua's men weren't. They stumbled and struggled, but their victories far outnumbered their defeats.

Canaan, then, does not represent the life to come. Canaan represents the life we can have now!

God invites us to enter Canaan. There is only one condition. We must turn our backs on the wilderness.

Just as Canaan represents the victorious Christian life, the wilderness represents the *defeated* Christian life. In the desert the Hebrew people were liberated from Egyptian bondage, but you wouldn't have known it by listening to them. Just three days into their freedom "the people complained against Moses, saying, 'What shall we drink?'" (Ex. 15:24).

A few more days passed, and "the children of Israel complained against Moses and Aaron in the wilderness . . . 'Oh, that we had died by the hand of the LORD in the land of Egypt . . . For you have brought us out into this wilderness to kill this whole assembly with hunger'" (16:2–3).

"The people contended with Moses" (17:2), and "the people complained against Moses" (v. 3). They inhaled anxiety like oxygen. They bellyached to the point that Moses prayed, "What shall I do with this people? They are almost ready to stone me!" (v. 4).

How did the Hebrews descend to this point? It wasn't for the lack of miracles. They saw God's power in high definition. They watched locusts gobble crops, boils devour skin, flies buzz through Pharaoh's court. God turned the chest-thumping Egyptians into shark bait right before the Hebrews' eyes. But when God called them to cross over into Canaan, the twelve spies returned, and all but two said the mission was impossible. The giants were too big for them. "We were like grasshoppers," they said (Num. 13:33). *We were tiny, tiny bugs. They will squash us.*

So God gave them time to think it over. He put the entire nation in time-out for nearly forty years. They walked in circles. They ate the same food every day. Life was an endless routine of the same rocks, lizards, and snakes. Victories were scarce. Progress was slow. They were saved but not strong. Redeemed but not released. Saved from Pharaoh but stuck in the desert. Redeemed but locked in a routine. Monotonous. Dull. Ho-hum, humdrum. Four decades of tedium.

Sounds miserable.

It might sound familiar.

I sat across the lunch table today from a man in midlife misery. He described his life with words like *stuck*, *rut*, and *stalled out*. He's a Christian. He can tell you the day he escaped Egypt. But he can't tell you the last time he defeated a temptation or experienced an answered prayer. Twenty years into his faith he fights the same battles he was fighting the day he came to Christ. He's out of Egypt, but Egypt's not out of him.

He didn't say the words, but I could sense the sentiment: "I thought the Christian life would be better than this." He feels disengaged and discouraged. It's as if the door to spiritual growth has a lock and everyone has the key but him. He doesn't know whom to blame. Himself? The church? God? He doesn't know what to do. Change congregations? Change Bible translations? Slow down and reflect? Get busy and work?

My friend is not alone in the wilderness. The REVEAL Research Project went on a search for Joshuas. Beginning in 2007 they surveyed the members of more than a thousand churches. They wanted to determine the percentage of churchgoers who are actually propelled by their faith to love God and love others with their whole hearts. How many Christians would describe their days as Glory Days?

The answer? Eleven percent.[4]

Eleven percent! Nearly nine out of ten believers, in other words, languish in the wilderness. Saved? Yes. Empowered? No. They waste away in the worst of ways—in the Land of In-Between. Out of Egypt but not yet in Canaan.

Eleven percent! If a high school graduated only 11 percent of its students, if a hospital healed only 11 percent of its patients, if a baseball team won only 11 percent of its games, if a home builder completed only 11 percent of his projects, wouldn't changes be made?

---

4. REVEAL Spiritual Life Survey database 2007–2014. For more information on the REVEAL Survey see Greg L. Hawkins and Cally Parkinson, *Move: What 1,000 Churches Reveal About Spiritual Growth* (Grand Rapids, MI: Zondervan, 2011).

The church has a serious deficiency.

We also have a wonderful opportunity. About 2.2 billion people on our planet call themselves Christians. That is approximately one-third of the world's population.[5] If the survey is any indication, about 2 billion of those Christians are chugging along on a fraction of their horsepower. Such sluggishness can only lead to weak churches and halfhearted ministries. What would happen if they got a tune-up? How would the world be different if 2 billion people came out of the wilderness? How much joy would be unleashed into the atmosphere? How much wisdom would be quarried and shared? How many marriages would be saved? How many wars would be prevented? How much hunger would be eliminated? How many orphanages would be built? How many orphanages would we need? If every Christian began to live the Promised Land life, how would the world be different?

If you began to live the Promised Land life, how would you be different? Do you sense a disconnect between the promises of the Bible and the reality of your life? Jesus offers abundant joy. Yet you live with oppressive grief. The epistles speak of grace. You shoulder such guilt. We are "more than conquerors" (Rom. 8:37) yet are commonly conquered by temptations or weaknesses.

Caught in the land between Egypt and Canaan.

Think about the Christian you want to be. What qualities do you want to have? More compassion? More conviction? More courage? What attitudes do you want to discontinue? Greed? Guilt? Endless negativity? A critical spirit?

Here is the good news. You can. With God's help you can close the gap between the person you are and the person you want to be, indeed, the person God made you to be. You can live "from glory to glory" (2 Cor. 3:18). The walls of Jericho are already condemned. The giants are already on the run. The deed to your new life in Canaan has already been signed. It just falls to you to possess the land.

---

5. "The Global Religious Landscape," Pew Research Religion & Public Life Project, December 18, 2012, www.pewforum.org/2012/12/18/global-religious-landscape-exec/.

Joshua and his men did this. They went from dry land to the Promised Land, from manna to feasts, from arid deserts to fertile fields. They inherited their inheritance. Their epitaph deserves a second reading.

> So the LORD gave to Israel all the land of which He had sworn to give to their fathers, and they took possession of it and dwelt in it. The LORD gave them rest all around, according to all that He had sworn to their fathers. And not a man of all their enemies stood against them; the LORD delivered all their enemies into their hand. Not a word failed of any good thing which the LORD had spoken to the house of Israel. All came to pass. (Josh. 21:43–45)

Personalize that promise. Put your name in the blanks.

> The Lord gave to _____ all the life he had sworn to give. And _____ took possession of it and dwelt in it. The Lord gave _____ rest all around and not an enemy stood. Not a word failed of any good thing which the Lord had spoken to _____. All came to pass.

This is God's vision for your life. Imagine the thought. You at full throttle. You as you were intended. You as victor over the Jerichos and giants.

You and your Promised Land life.

It is yours for the taking.

Expect to be challenged. The enemy won't go down without a fight. But expect great progress. Life is different on the west side of the Jordan. Breakthroughs outnumber breakdowns. God's promises outweigh personal problems. Victory becomes, dare we imagine, a way of life. Isn't it time for you to change your mailing address from the wilderness to the Promised Land? Your Glory Days await you.

Ready to march?